A Recipe for Healing

Other books in the Mind Diet Journaling Program and how to order them:

Count Your Life With Smiles, Not Tears
ISBN: 0-9720605-0-2

Healing From Within, Emotionally Surviving Cancer
ISBN 0-9720605-1-0

Beyond Valentine's Day, Making Love All Year Long
ISBN 0-9720605-2-9

You may purchase these books at www.minddietbooks.com or any retail book outlet. For information on upcoming books, speaking engagements, and to ask questions of the author, please visit our Web site:

www.minddietbooks.com

A Recipe for Healing

Coming Together as a Team

STEVE JAFFE

THE MIND DIET GROUP

10 9 8 7 6 5 4 3 2 1

A Mind Diet Journaling Series® Book
Published by: The Mind Diet Group, Inc.
Carlsbad, California
Phone: 760-436-7253 Fax: 760-436-6608
E-mail: Minddietbooks@aol.com
www.minddietbooks.com

PUBLISHER'S CATALOGING-IN-PUBLICATION DATA
Jaffe, Steve.
A recipe for healing : coming together as a team / Steve Jaffe.
p. cm.
ISBN 0-9720605-6-1
Library of Congress Control Number: 2003114553
[1. Cancer—Patients—Family relationships.
2. Cancer—Psychological aspects. 3. Cancer—Patients—Poetry.
4. Diaries—Authorship.] I. Title.
RC262 .J34 2004
362.1/96994—dc22 CIP

Printed and bound in the United States of America

Cover Design and Text Layout by: To The Point Solutions
www.tothepointsolutions.com

To my wife, Nancy, who has taught me how to be an important part of her constant recovery. Beating her cancer has truly been, and remains, a powerful team effort on both our parts.

And to all the men who have shared their fears and confusion about their partners' cancer and their desire to help the women they love not feel alone. This book is dedicated to all of you. Please help other men who are going through what you have experienced.

CONTENTS

Section 2

Section 3

Section 4

Section 7

A Message From the Author

I have been asked numerous times why I created The Mind Diet™ Journaling Series. Although my answer has changed frequently, the reason I've given most often is that I needed a simple and easy method to solve the many problems that entered my life on a daily basis.

As I evolved —as this series evolved—I realized that I desperately needed a motivating, sincere, and honest coach in my life. I read hundreds of self-help books, attended numerous motivational seminars, and purchased enough tapes and CDs promising solutions to improve my life that I could have bought a luxury car that would have given me just as much pleasure.

The bottom line was that I needed to discover who I was and what I wanted to be. That's when I decided the best coach, mentor, advisor, and sage was ME. At first, taking on this responsibility was scary, but once it happened, a world of possibilities opened up and barriers and obstacles that had once held me back were destroyed.

Relationships were never meant to be easy. In fact, relationships are often the most challenging and important issues in our lives. It doesn't matter what stage your relationship is in at this time, working as a team is essential if you want to live happily with someone. You cannot predict what obstacles will befall a marriage or a committed relationship, including a life-threatening illness.

How you cope and deal with the illness, whether it's yours or a loved one's is critical if you want the relationship to survive. Once a life-threatening disease enters your life and your significant relationship(s), you need to find that special strength that is dormant inside your heart and mind, so you can recover fully, both physically and emotionally.

When a serious disease enters your life, it is time for open and honest communication, to enable you to get through all the stages of the illness that lie ahead. You will have to believe that the impossible is possible, and to embrace and love the changes that come with the disease. How you allow the disease to affect those around you, especially your loved ones, is critical.

The ability to communicate honestly can be the most difficult part of the recovery process, since it is normal to not want to burden a loved one, even yourself, with the horrible thoughts that can fester inside your mind each day, torturing your spirit.

During the last five years I have dealt with my heart disease and my wife's breast cancer, by learning to change patterns of behavior so we could work together as a strong team. Our relationship changed the moment breast cancer entered our lives and continued to change after I was diagnosed with coronary artery disease. Our love for each other, however, did not diminish. It got stronger because we learned how to communicate and express our true emotions.

I was not prepared to deal with the heart disease and cancer that hit us within a six-month period. Even to this day I hate taking a nitro tablet in front of my wife and see her look of worry and concern. When I notice fatigue overwhelm her or she gets a nosebleed for no apparent reason, fear and anxiety strike me hard and chest pains return, putting me on the roller coaster ride of not knowing what to say or do without worrying her. At moments like this I am glad I have my journaling technique to vent my frustrations and to come up with the logical answers I need in order to cope.

I am not implying that you don't express the feelings stirring around inside your head and heart, but through examples in this book I show you how to overcome these obstacles to self-expression. Additionally, while this book focuses on how illness affects relationships, the journaling process you learn will spill over into other aspects of your life.

Discovering the reasons that prevent you from speaking from your heart is the first step in experiencing happiness and pleasure during difficult and stressful times.

To benefit the most from this book you will have to be ready to uncover and understand the real you. You will have to look beyond your partner and be willing to make life-altering evaluations about yourself. You must be willing to find and reevaluate that private person who is you through journaling.

Journaling is a medically proven method of reclaiming your life and getting in control of what is truly healthy for you. *A Recipe For Healing, Coming Together As A Team* was written to be one of many tools to keep your marriage, or other significant relationships, strong during trying circumstances.

The first few chapters of this book will expose you to strong, emotionally stirring poems that were inspired by my personal experiences and from other survivors who faced similar anxieties and frustrations during their recovery from a serious illness or loss, including divorce.

As you go through the book, you will work as an individual and as a couple, with the intention of exposing your emotions in a safe and nurturing environment. It is the hidden truths that stay blocked and buried away that cause the beginnings of friction in a once cohesive relationship. To begin to heal, you must be willing to allow your thoughts and feelings to flow out of your head and onto paper. That is what this interactive journaling program has been designed to accomplish.

You will find a way to communicate your emotions with your spouse, or significant other, so that as a couple each of you can hear and understand the true feelings of fear and anxiety that have been stored and locked inside your heart and mind.

When one person in a relationship gets a serious disease such as cancer, heart disease, stroke, or any one of a thousand other devastating illnesses, the relationship instantly changes. Most people dislike change and cannot cope or adjust properly to it. This is when the two of you have to discover a means to honestly communicate in order to prevent negative feelings from festering and building into problems that can eventually become too large to solve.

The poems in the beginning of this book were written after I interviewed cancer and heart disease survivors who faced divorce or who had been divorced as a consequence of their illness. I know it sounds heartless that anyone would divorce a loved one in a time of need, but it is a tragic reality that needs intervention.

This interactive journaling book is that intervention. You might find some of the poems a bit strong and disturbing, which is what I intended to accomplish, so both of you can be honest and admit that all or part of each poem reflects a hidden truth about your current feelings.

Once you've mastered the ability to open up, to not be afraid, and to be vulnerable to your partner, the warm connection of love will begin to blanket your body and entwine your mind and spirit as one. Once you commit to this process, then and only then can you move toward a full emotional recovery from the illness that is consuming your life.

I have seen remarkable results from cancer and heart disease survivors who have used this journaling series, and challenge you to give a one hundred percent of yourself to the techniques you are about to learn. Realize, though, that for the journaling techniques to work, you have to commit to keeping an open mind and also have a desire to view your life from a different perspective.

Both people in the relationship are experiencing similar emotions about the disease that has entered your lives. *A Recipe For Healing, Coming Together As A Team* can be the healing companion that will keep your marriage and personal relationships strong during these difficult times.

In times of stress and challenge people sometimes forget how to be happy, inventive, creative, and healthy. Realize you have the power to teach yourself how to go back to that "happy zone" you experienced before

I intend for the Mind Diet Journaling Series to teach everyone how to embrace change by writing rhythm poetry. That is my ultimate goal, but it is the *process* not the *product* that will make this journaling series meaningful. Too often, people resist change or refuse to deal with it. What you discover inside this book will help you embrace change and eventually love it.

Your desire to write rhythm poetry or to express your emotions in writing, will trigger inquisitiveness for self-inquiry and self-direction, something both of you desperately need.

Before you embark on a magical journey that will forever change the way you see your partner, here is one last point I want to make. Men and women go through The Mind Diet Series differently and have their own way of looking at a situation. It is your job to understand your partner's differences and to embrace them, and to realize that it is you who needs to change, not your partner.

ABOUT THE AUTHOR

Poetry saved my life. You might think I mean this in some lofty, metaphorical way, but I don't. I mean it literally.

My heart gave out in 1999. After three angioplasties and finally a quadruple bypass, my doctors prescribed the only thing that would cure me: I needed to relax. At the time, however, that was impossible. I was in a nasty, expensive legal battle with my former employer; my oldest child was seriously ill; and I was still reeling from a spiteful divorce from my wife of twenty-one years. But worse than all of that, my new wife—a ray of sunlight in the darkness—had just been diagnosed with breast cancer. I felt like things were coming at me from every angle and I couldn't get out from underneath the burden.

As it turns out, the stress was not only impeding my recovery, it was also contributing to my illness. In a study by The British National Health, Safety and Environmental Department, stress accounts for eighty percent of most modern illnesses, especially heart disease. Another alarming statistic, from a study by the American Institute of Stress, found that seventy to ninety percent of visits to primary care physicians were for stress related problems. In a very real way, stress was killing me—and I didn't know how to turn off the valve.

Even though the solution to my health problem was to relax, none of my doctors had a workable answer as to how I should accomplish this. I tried meditation, long walks, and exercise. I even sold my businesses and retired. Changing my lifestyle was not working. My chest pains continued to get stronger and stronger.

Although I'd always kept a journal, what I was writing in it—my anger and frustration—was negative. One day, however, as I wrote about the arrogant attitude of the claims adjuster who had denied part of my claim, I noticed something magical happening. My thoughts started to dance as I wrote, turning my emotions into, for lack of a better word, poetry. Now, I'm not claiming to be the next William Shakespeare, but the melodic, rhyming stanzas started to do what no doctor, no medication, and no quadruple bypass had been able to. They provided relief and even solutions to the severe problems that were plaguing me—strike that—killing me.

Each time I finished a poem, I felt better. As one poem turned into twenty, I felt a change blanketing my body. The stressful thoughts that weighed on me for so long and controlled my chest pains were now channeled into this newfound journaling technique I called "rhythm poetry."

Writing rhythm poetry forced me to shine a bright light on my life and take an honest look at the choices I'd made. And yes, that was often unpleasant. Think about how leeches were used in medieval times to suck infections out of wounds. Same idea. The poems were able to release the poisonous emotions, giving my brain a reprieve. I coined the term "mind diet," because this regime was making my mind fit and healthy, and in turn, having a similar effect on my body.

Even experts agree the key to good health and healing is learning to honestly identify your feelings—something few of us are able to do well. "The written word is very powerful," says Dr. John Graham-Pole, a professor of pediatrics and affiliate professor of clinical psychology at the University of Florida. "It helps (people) to make sense of things that are otherwise hard to make sense of." Writing rhythm poems forced me to address the crazy thoughts, worries, anxieties, tensions, and fears I'd been living with for years.

What I was doing, I realize now, was telling *Me* about myself—my hidden feelings—through my poems. I had allowed my life to revolve around others, while I neglected myself and kept the stress bottled up inside. Rhythm poetry opened up my mind to possibilities that had previously seemed impossible.

Before I began to write poetry, there were mornings I hid in bed rather than confront the myriad of problems awaiting me. I remember one morning lying in bed, thinking about the day ahead of me: my wife was scheduled for a radiation treatment, my child had gone off his meds for the fourth time, and a team of contentious lawyers was planning to eat me for lunch at a deposition. But instead of burrowing under my blankets, I wrote a poem called "Stay Loose." I used the page to deal with my inability to cope at that moment.

Stay Loose

The storm is here.
The wind is blowing,
trying to knock me down.
I am prepared to brace myself,
with feet well-planted on the ground.
I will stay loose and not fall down,
these storms all seem to burn out.

I will just try to stand my ground,
and pound my chest and shout:
"You might be big and you might be strong.
I am not scared or blue.
So blow real hard and try your best,
your time has run out for you."

The poem is simple, short, and about something tangible that was happening at that moment in my life. It helped me face the day.

I have soldiered through many other bleak days, armed with nothing but rhythm poetry. I kept writing until my mind was free of all unwanted thoughts. During my wife's battle with breast cancer I wrote a group of poems that are now included in *Healing From Within, Emotionally Surviving Cancer.* Writing those poems saved me from complete despair. The poems, "Go Away I'm Not Home," "Day by Day," and "Hope in Small Bunches" are just a few of the ninety-plus poems I wrote during that time. They helped me deal with my emotions, rather than letting them fester. Writing rhythm poetry gave me an incredibly powerful feeling.

To share that power with others, I created the The Mind Diet Series™ (information about the program can be found at www.minddietbooks.com). This interactive journaling program provides step-by-step instruction on how to unleash your healing abilities. So far, I've released three books: *Count Your Life With Smiles, Not Tears*, *Healing From Within, Emotionally Surviving Cancer*, and *Beyond Valentine's Day, Making Love All Year Long*. Each book tackles a different subject, but uses the same therapeutic techniques.

The most important thing to remember about writing rhythm poetry: it doesn't require a writing lesson. It does, however, require a desire on your part to want to be healthy every day and heal the daily ills that are plaguing you.

My series is about the process, not the product.

Perhaps the most important part of The Mind Diet technique is the personal evaluation sheet. In order to change, reduce your stress, and improve your health, you first have to deal with all the factors that encompass your life. Make a list of twenty desires, attributes, and qualities you want for yourself. Make sure you're being honest and open-minded. These descriptions have to be exactly what you have always wanted. Then rate each one on a scale of one to five (five being the highest) and add up your score. You should strive to be somewhere between eighty-five and ninety-five percent on your evaluation sheet. What you have accomplished is a mental and written picture of who you are going to become. (I am still working on mine, by the way.)

It was through this exercise that during my darkest times, I discovered I was not the person I wanted to be. I was molding myself into what I thought the world around me wanted. Every day I woke and saw a stranger in the mirror. Until I decided to change, to take control, and become the real me—nothing else I was doing to mend my health would work. Slowly, I started to shed away years and years of habits, personality traits, and relationship ruts I had always fallen back into.

In order to sculpt the person you'd like to see each day, you have to be willing to scrutinize your own insecurities, fears, phobias, habits, and current relationships.

After you've completed the evaluation, you'll read some of my poems to get an idea of how to go about writing rhythm poetry. Then you'll begin to write your own poems. The process is easy and doesn't require that you have any creative talent. Once you've identified the feelings or emotions you care to write about, you choose a title—this is possibly the most important step in writing the poem. The title expresses your emotions, feelings, and anxieties at the moment. After determining a title, the rhythm poem just flows out of your brain onto the paper. At first you might write only a few lines, however as you become more comfortable, you will begin to witness your poems getting longer with more detailed solutions.

The key to this journaling technique is to be sure you write a message to yourself and end each poem with a positive affirmation or solution. Do not think that you can solve your problems by writing to change others—I've tried, and believe me, it only brings greater frustration and avoidance of the real problems. If you're able to help yourself, then you can sit back and watch your world change for the better.

Happiness is the goal. Liking yourself is the first step in the process. Writing rhythm poetry for health and healing will be painful and overwhelming at first. Accepting your own faults is never easy. However, as you work on your flaws, you will begin to see celebration in your world. Your poems will provide you with a written blueprint to guide you through your metamorphosis.

I have enjoyed coaching others and teaching them how to write through painful emotions and learning to love change. As you write poetry to inspire yourself, you are on the road to a well-balanced life that will keep you healthy for many years.

While Eastern medicine is just beginning to explore the mind/body connection, the use of poetry as medicine goes back to ancient Egypt and beyond. "Poetry and medicine are so closely intertwined," says Jack Coulehan, MD, MPH, director of the institute for Medicine in Contemporary Society at State University of New York at Stony Brook. "When you go back in history and think about how healing occurred in traditional societies, most healing was related to the power of the word."

I'm living proof that this is true. These days, my heart is healthy and my spirit is happy. Life is good. Thanks to poetry. I'd like to end with a poem that explains what a Mind Diet can be for you.

A Mind Diet

A mind diet is the sunrise each morning,
and the sunset every night,
A mind diet reduces the stressful weight,
that is inside you and squeezing too tight.

A mind diet is a warm hug from your love,
or the praise that is given when you feel so unloved.
A mind diet releases the many things stuffed inside our heads
helping us to be able to jump out of bed.

The stresses of life are with us all the time,
making our minds overweight,
we need a constant mind diet to level us out,
before it becomes too late.

A program to reduce the weight that you carry,
requires that you diet well,
and work on the mind that is stressed so hard,
with an agenda for mind re-sell.

A mind diet is your way to release
and also your way to cope,
a mind diet only works for you,
if you truly attempt to invoke.

What is needed to lose all this unwanted weight,
is to open and express what's inside.
This release frees up all of the bulk,
that keeps brewing, and trying to desperately hide.

So commit to this diet,
that will reduce all this weight,
and allow you to feel a Mind Diet state.
A Mind Diet is the first step for you,
to bring out a beautiful much brighter view.

Steve Jaffe is a published poet and novelist and has been featured on more than one hundred radio and TV programs, as well as being reviewed in newspapers in the United States, Canada, United Kingdom, and Australia. His article "Poetry for Health and Healing" appeared in the May 2003 issue of *Positive Health* magazine in the United Kingdom.

He graduated from California State University at Pomona with a Bachelor of Science degree in marketing.He has owned an insurance agency and a direct mail advertising company. Prior to those careers he worked in the corporate world for an oil company.

In 1999 he retired due to health reasons.

While using poetry to heal his heart disease, he created The Mind Diet Group, Inc., which publishes interactive journaling books in the Mind Diet™ Journaling Series. The series presently consists of three books: *Count Your Life With Smiles, Not Tears*; *Healing From Within, Emotionally Surviving Cancer*; and *Beyond Valentine's Day, Making Love All Year Long*.

"When I discovered the power of my 'rhythm poetry' and saw how it benefited others trying to cope with life's daily pressures, I decided to share my poetry so I could help make a difference in our ever-changing world."

For more information about this series go to
www.minddiet.com

A Note to Survivors and Their Partners

A devastating illness or loss will leave a mark that will forever stay with you. How you go about dealing with life-altering situations is the focus of this journaling book.

Can couples celebrate life or will they have visions of devastation? Consumption of the disease can fill the survivor and the spouse (or significant other) with isolation; an overwhelming strain on coping skills and an immediate change within the relationship will occur—like an unannounced tornado. The first knee-jerk reaction is to keep feelings locked inside, hiding your fears and troubles. While this type of thinking is noble, it will keep both of you guessing what the other person is feeling. You need to venture outside the comfort zone you've withdrawn into and find new, healthy ways to manage your stress.

Keeping your emotions locked inside will make you ill. Letting feelings flow out with meaning will begin the healing process. While the survivor has the toughest part of dealing with the illness, the spouse has to learn a new role in a once stable family unit: that of caregiver.

Why would anyone want to express his or her feelings on paper, journaling privately, writing words that seem to talk to the writer? The simplest answer I can provide is that by writing down your feelings, you are delegating the building pressures inside your head to paper, allowing a meditative release of unwanted stress. If you have a tendency to keep things bottled up, one day your cup will run over, affecting the dynamics of your relationship.

The meaning and the tone of the word *cancer*, for example, affects couples differently. They understand and express themselves from different points of view. The squeezing out of feelings can become difficult, causing a strain where there should be compassion and understanding. During the recovery period, which is unfortunately forever, a meaningful method of expression has to take place between the two people affected by this illness. This form of communication has to become a habit that is practiced daily.

I had been expressing my feelings long before my wife's cancer diagnosis entered our lives over five years ago. I had learned how to express my feelings without the stigma it has for some men. If you are a spouse reading this book, you must love your partner very much. Your Survivor is a unique person, who needs all the love and support you can muster, as he or she tries to fight the death sentence that races inside his or her mind each day. The survivor's thoughts not only have to deal with the medical treatments to fight the disease, but also the mental torment of not knowing what tomorrow might bring.

Cancer has not been cured, heart disease can be slowly reversed, and other illnesses can linger for years, disrupting the lives of everyone touched by the survivor. What should you do as emotions spin out of control? My only answer is that you should talk and let go of the horrific feelings that are blocked and unable to pass through your lips. Unfortunately, what has come easy for me is not universally easy for others. This is where The Mind Diet Journaling Program intervenes and guides you through a series of emotionally stirring poems.

The desired outcome is not for you to just read the poems, but to also express your feelings—fear, hopelessness, sorrow, tension, and pain—in a special dance of words that will communicate to your partner your love and empathy. It is the honest and painful emotional expressions that will bond you with your partner during this period.

Most of the cancer survivors I have spoken to or seen since May 1998 portray a special bond with other survivors and especially with themselves. Seeing the outer shell of the survivor can be very misleading. Most survivors put on a positive, healthy appearance in their daily routines, and it becomes confusing and sometimes bewildering to believe they have cancer. The person without cancer starts to believe that he/she sees someone who is truly cured of the disease. This is the hard part for all spouses. After a point in time, we think our lives can get back to "normal." As a man, I have always wanted an objective way to find fixes to problems. Cancer is not an objective disease, and doesn't have a quick fix.

The passion, the spontaneity, and the way couples had once made love will change. It is a sad fact, but not a hopeless one. It doesn't mean the marriage or relationship is over.

Men have to take on a different role. One we might not be prepared for or even know how to do. We have to become the primary caregiver of the family unit. All the previous caregiver's energy (the survivor) is now being directed into staying alive.

Does this mean you'll never have the marriage you had fantasized about? No. It means that your relationship has to mature to a new level and you (the spouse/significant other) must become proactive in making that happen.

How can poetry accomplish this enormous feat? For centuries, poetry has been one of the few communicative arts to bring out the truth in one's heart. The Mind Diet Journaling Program focuses on bringing out the honest expression of feelings that are not surfacing. If emotions are left in our minds to ferment, they will fester and cause a giant wedge to form within the relationship.

If you follow the program in this book, you will see your humanness materialize before your eyes. You will discover what life is really about. You will fall in love once again, possibly with a stronger friendship that will hold your relationship together for the rest of your lives.

As you begin the Mind Diet Journaling Program, be honest with your emotions, no matter how painful this might be at first. Through honest communication and understanding, love will blossom. I have shared my journey through my poems, exposing who I am to a world of strangers, which for me has been the most frightening experience of my life.

On May 12, 1998, my wife, Nancy, was told she had breast cancer. For a woman who had been healthy all of her life, took wonderful care of herself, and had no family history of this disease well, needless to say, she was devastated. I knew Nancy would have liked to have buried her head in the sand and pretend that the most horrible phrase in the English language, "You have cancer," had never been said to her. However, she couldn't and neither could I.

I knew she would have wanted to handle this on her own. Nancy is very independent and never tries to burden others with her problems. But, she was not the only one affected by the cancer—I was, too. An enemy had attacked my beautiful, loving, and caring best friend, an enemy I could not protect her from.

Hopelessness does not describe what I felt when her surgeon advised me that her lump looked cancerous. Shock, anger, desperation, and wondering how I could help raced through my mind like a cyclone. The surgeon was no help.

As soon as I saw Nancy in recovery, I knew I had found my answer. She had a bright smile that lit up her face and that's when I knew how I was going to help her.

While I couldn't remove the mind-set that "cancer meant death," I began to realize that death in her case would not come immediately. I started to read as much as I could about breast cancer and all the treatments and postoperative affects cancer would have on her. I supported Nancy when she spent time away from me at cancer retreats. Acknowledging that there would be changes in our relationship, allowed me to find the sweet lemonade that would pull us through amongst the sour lemons life had dealt us..

I wrote my first series of poems entitled, "Go Away I'm Not Home," and "Emotionally Surviving Cancer: A Mind Diet," as a gift for her. It started out as a series of poems I wrote that helped me get into her shoes and walk side-by-side, holding the cancer in my hands. Nancy surprised me when she shared these poems with thirty cancer survivors on a Healing Odyssey Retreat in Santa Barbara in April 1999. I was astonished to learn how my personal poems touched these breast cancer survivors. Subsequently, through much prodding and positive encouragement from these courageous women, the Mind Diet Journaling Series was born. The original book, now titled *Healing From Within, Emotionally Surviving Cancer*, is the evolution of something that started from diversity and ended in a celebration about life.

As a man, husband, and friend to a woman I plan on spending eternity with, I want to share my understanding, compassion, and experience with other people and their survivors in this new journaling book, A *Recipe For Healing, Coming Together As A Team*. No matter what emotional state you are presently in, learning to confront your demons is the first step on the long and wonderful journey to live each day to its fullest.

Spouses and significant others, open your hearts and let your emotions flow toward the beautiful and courageous survivor who is now growing into a treasure of audacity, hope, and resolve in her/his fight to survive. She/he needs you more than ever. She/he is not abandoning you, but trying to save a life that she/he so desperately wants to keep sharing with you.

Now is the time for you to become stronger than you have ever been. With teamwork and understanding, this part of your life will grow into a deeper and to a more passionate level. Don't abandon her/him when she/he needs you more than ever.

Beginning Exercise

Before you proceed to the next section, I'd like both of you to do a simple exercise to start the journaling mind-set. On a separate sheet of paper each of you should list ten things you love about your spouse or significant other. When both of you have completed the lists, read them to each other. You should begin to feel a stirring of emotions, which is what you are trying to accomplish when you begin to read the rhythm poems and write out your feelings about how the poems affected you.

What you should be feeling is what I call "A Mind Diet"—the emotional release that makes you feel good. To make this journaling program work effectively, don't hold back. Let your emotions and tears flow.

A Message From Nancy Jaffe

Cancer was a shock to me. I wasn't ready. I had a busy, productive life—I had plans. I just didn't have time for it.

Eventually reality set in. I became confused and couldn't think straight. I was preoccupied with thoughts of death. The extra "weight" in my head and on my shoulders was crushing me. My entire world was turned upside down.

Although I was smiling and positive on the outside, wanting to appear strong, I was scared to death on the inside.

My husband, Steve, saw right through me. He recognized my uncertainty and my fight to hold onto my independence. He talked to me, he asked me questions, he provided the strength and support I needed—so that I wouldn't go through my cancer journey alone.

He started writing poems for me. He was actually writing in the FIRST PERSON, as if he were going though the diagnosis, treatment, recovery, and changes. Through his rhythm poetry I realized that he truly understood and felt my fear. His poems offered me a sense of empowerment. The hope, confidence, faith, and support that were embedded in his poetry transported those feelings into my being.

Steve's encouragement through my cancer diagnosis, treatment, and recovery helped me identify what was truly important in life: not material things—but love, trust, hope, and health.

Every moment is precious, and every day Steve and I remind each other how blessed we are to be together.

Introduction to the Mind Diet Philosophy

To explain what a MIND DIET is would be like trying to describe a beautiful sunset or a warm hug or a nonstop belly laugh. It is difficult to find the exact words to define a Mind Diet because a Mind Diet is an individual experience. It is something that begins inside your brain and controls every part of your body. How you experience a Mind Diet may not be the same as your spouse/significant other or me.

To give you a starting point, let me try to define what a Mind Diet is for me. Realize, however, your definition will expand as you become more involved in your search.

> **MIND DIET:** The precise moment when your mind and body quiver, you get goose bumps, your thoughts get lost in the moment, and a rush of exhilarated emotions takes over—simultaneously.

Each person experiences life's thrills from different perspectives. Can you recall a wonderful occasion or moment when a rush of adrenaline swept over your body for a split second? Did you smile, laugh, or cry for joy? Did it feel great to communicate your feelings with someone who understood you, the moment you realized someone was listening? Or did you witness a sunrise or a sunset and feel a warm stillness flow through your body? Those are all MIND DIETS!

Should you strive to experience A MIND DIET every moment of your life? I think so! And I believe that it should be written down with a dancing of words. As you write your own rhythm poems you will begin to feel a special tingling blanket your body. It is the beginning of a Mind Diet.

Initially, writing alone is acceptable, but when you have the opportunity to share these moments with someone special, your feelings will be unmatched by anything you have ever felt. Putting your feelings into a paragraph, writing a whole page, or creating a rhythm poem are wonderful gifts that need to be shared. Everyone has a need to communicate, so why not do it with a Mind Diet of feelings and emotions with someone dear?

Not every day will be a Mind Diet type of day. Unfortunately, life just won't allow this to happen. Your day-to-day problems, moods, or your body chemistry won't let your mind release you from some painful moments. In my considered opinion, you should not avoid those difficult times. Burying your head in the sand only delays having to deal with life. Problems, pain, fear, and loss will not go away by escaping. Some people turn to alcohol, cigarettes, and drugs as a Mind Diet to relieve their problems. These solutions, however, only compound the difficulties that plague you.

Life is like a wheel

Picture your life as a wheel, with as many spokes as you require to keep the wheel rounded. Visualize each spoke as representing everything good and bad in your life. Once you see the current factors that sum up your life, then you can find the weak spokes that need improvement, so your wheel will roll smoothly on your journey. The main purpose of this book is to help couples find the weak spokes that the survivor and spouse have pertaining to the illness or loss that has affected their lives.

You will change as you practice the Mind Diet Journaling Program. You will feel some of your weak spokes become healthier and more positive. As this happens, your wheel will become steadier and will roll down your pathway more smoothly, allowing you to be stronger for your partner.

When you are subjected to unpleasant periods in your life, finding Mind Diet experiences will bring more beneficial events to the surface to get absorbed into your life. You will begin to see and celebrate yourself more clearly by developing a certain rhythm that allows you to deal with everyday life, including a serious illness.

The heart of this book is to use rhythm poetry to strengthen who you are and to help you deal with everyday life. The title of the book, *A Recipe For Healing: Coming Together As A Team,* truly explains what my desire is for each of you. You have only this life to make the most out of, and right now is the best time to begin to re-invent that new relationship that is shaping itself around you.

The poems in this book have been designed to motivate and stimulate your mind and thoughts. They will help you communicate, first with yourself, and then with your spouse, a best friend, or someone else who is dear to you.

They are only examples. Eventually, you will develop a magical rhythm and you'll be able to journal your own poems to release your feelings. Remember: Don't worry about having an instant rhythm at first?it will come as your mind begins to lose its excess weight.

Suggestions on completing the program

The Mind Diet Journaling Program has been designed to allow you as much time as necessary to work on each chapter. Each assignment is short and easy to follow. First you will read the assigned poems, and then you'll practice them for as long as necessary, expressing what each poem meant to you during every difficult or pleasant situation you saw yourself in at that moment. You will journal how you felt during each experience. At first, you will just write your feelings. Then, as you become more comfortable writing, you will find your rhythm and watch a poem that expresses how you felt bloom before your eyes. Another important tip to remember is that there may be a point in your life when you need to go back to a poem that fits into your life circumstance at that moment. It is perfectly okay to use more than one poem to help you at any point in time.

One last and crucial point I need to mention before you start on your Mind Diet journaling is that this book's focus is to help you and you alone, as you struggle to cope with your pain and sorrow. If you write from that viewpoint, then this journaling process will work. Do not try to use this tool to change your spouse or anyone else who might have an investment in your recovery. Change will happen without it being forced.

The book is written to help you change and to see your world with glowing eyes. Your only aspiration is to make a better you. Then all else will fall into place.

I wish you the best during your life. Remember:

You CAN work as a team when adversity enters your lives.

How Mind Diet Journaling Works

Your first attempt at the Mind Diet journaling program will be private. While you can read the poems together, with your spouse or significant other, you might feel more at ease going somewhere alone to write your thoughts after you've jotted down some feelings that have been stirred. It is perfectly acceptable to write about your emotions (your poems) and not share them right away. As you begin to understand yourself and how the illness is affecting you, then you can listen with an open heart to your partner's emotions.

If communication before the disease or loss was difficult, uncomfortable, or nonexistent, patience and understanding will have to be granted when you start this new method of relating with each other. I suggest that you find a quiet time in your day to practice the journaling. If you both work outside the home, I suggest you wake up thirty minutes earlier than usual, use your lunch break, or write before dinner. The important thing is to make the time for this program. Then, as you become more comfortable expressing yourself, you can establish a place and time each day to read your rhythm poetry to your partner.

Don't feel inadequate if your partner picks up the rhythm part of writing faster than you. It doesn't mean they are more emotional or more in tune with what is going on. The ability to write your feelings down on a piece of paper is the accomplishment. Understand that it is the process, not the product, that you are shooting for.

A life-threatening illness has become a permanent boarder in your home. How you treat that boarder and the person affected will forever change your life. The Mind Diet Journaling Program works if you place your entire heart and soul into it. Be committed to seeing your life from new eyes and fall in love once again. Plan a life filled with Mind Diets every day.

Before you move on to the first chapter, let's first experiment with the existing emotions you have about the illness that has come into your life. Make a list of the first five things that come into your mind when you think about your loss or the disruption to your life and how you believe it is affecting both of you. List only the emotions that you imagine your partner is feeling.

Using this list, write a short paragraph about what you believe is going through your partner's head. Don't worry about creating a rhythm poem at this point. If you feel you can, then give it a try. Once this exercise is finished, try to verbalize to your significant other, from a place deep inside your heart, how you think you can help.

Section 1

Living with an Illness or Loss

Remission is a word we hope will be the cure-all for our worries. Unfortunately, remission is just a holding pattern we remain in for the rest of our lives. The focus of this book is on dealing with cancer and heart disease. If your relationship is suffering because of a different illness just substitute your disease for the ones mentioned in here.

There are many words and phrases that are said to us by people trying to lift our spirits. Nevertheless, the words that we never seem to hear are: *Your cancer is completely gone* or *You do not have heart disease anymore.*

Cancer and heart disease patients and their spouses live in a world of anxiety-riddled expectations. People who have suffered the loss of a loved one have their own emotions. One of the biggest complaints from cancer survivors is the fear of their illness returning, and of death. People who have suffered a loss cannot see a bright future and they dwell on their own unique pain.

Survivors have a commonality that links them as a special community. Most cancer survivors I have spoken with remain in a forced, enthusiastic state; masking inside their minds the worry and trepidation of when their personal lives will once again be touched by cancer. Anyone with heart disease is forced to be aware of every tiny change in his/her body. They feel things that most healthy people do not feel, which increases their anxiety that a heart attack or stroke is about to occur.

How can you cope with the most hideous word in the English language, cancer? Or deal with the knowledge that your heart is damaged? Or the expectation that once touched by loss, it will happen again if you open your emotional heart?

Support groups for cancer survivors (thank God there are many) provide the much-needed companionship a cancer survivor needs. There are not as many groups for men with heart disease. Hopefully one day soon, especially as more men learn to share their emotions, this will change. The type of support group that is needed is one for the spouses, significant others, and family members of these survivors.

In this book the term *spouse* will, in most cases, refer to husbands. Why husbands? They seem to be the one group that is most lost in what they can or are willing to do to support their wives during the struggle to overcome the thoughts of the illness or loss. Most men are not equipped to go from the emotional receiver to the emotional caregiver. Their normal lives will transform into a constant upheaval. The demands this strange, new role puts upon them will interfere with their occupation, their personal time, and most importantly, their intimacy with their wives.

The once comfortable family unit has now fallen victim to an irrational state of flux that keeps bearing toward a desolate state of affairs, which eventually strains the marriage/relationship immensely. What happens when the primary caregiver in a marriage is overcome by an illness? Can the spouse step in and assume the role of caregiver? In a lot of cases it does not happen. Not because a husband doesn't *want* to help, but because he does not know *how* to help.

From birth, few men are taught to be caregivers. In their parents' marriage they witnessed the role their mother played and when they are tossed into the "female" role, they become lost in a world that they do not have a rule book for.

Can a marriage survive when an illness or other loss moves in? I believe it can. At first it will be hard, but with a willingness to communicate, the process will move in a positive, forward direction.

The Mind Diet Series™ is a positive method to help couples survive during one of the most difficult situations they will ever face together: A life-threatening illness.

Through the writing of rhythmic poems, to the communication of your feelings about what you wrote, you will open up a special dialogue that will bring a new, beautiful, and emotional level to your relationships. You will both gain a special perspective on life and the relationship.

Some cancer survivors have said that their diagnosis was a gift. It taught them to view life from different eyes and create new beginnings before their candles burned out. As a survivor of heart disease, I too see my life as a gift, living it to the best of my abilities and opening new doors of opportunities that remained closed when I thought I was immortal.

This is a wonderful opportunity to find new beginnings in your marriage/relationship and to see the world of possibilities that is before you. Nothing has really changed, except a special opportunity for growth as a human being.

It is sad that it takes a life-threatening illness to open one's eyes. Open yours now. Time is ticking away. Stop seeing your life with regrets. Speak to each other honestly and, most of all, listen unconditionally.

Having a life-altering disease or suffering from a loss does not mean you cannot enjoy touching, comforting, and giving warmth to your wife. She has changed for the better, because she now sees you, herself, and your marriage with clear eyes. You need to do the same. You can remain best friends, lovers, and husband and wife.

Exercise

Before you read the rhythm poems in this chapter, write down the ten fears you have about the illness or loss, your marriage, your intimacy, and most of all, your spouse/partner.

My Fears:

1.
2.
3.
4.
5.
6.
7.
8.
9.
10.

Now read the following ten poems and write down your feelings, either in a paragraph or a rhythm poem format. It doesn't matter which style you choose at first. You will soon find that a special rhythm will blanket your body and guide you toward a happier marriage and A Mind Diet Experience.

What Did I Do Wrong?

How come I feel guilty with this disease inside my body?
I struggle with the pain.
Could I have done something else
and avoided this unfortunate shame?

I think of all the food I've eaten,
I toil with the thoughts of sin.
I wonder if God was listening
to the evil that flowed within.

I wish I had known if I had control
of the sickness that brewed inside,
I would have done anything to prevent
the curse that now controls my life.

What have I done wrong to deserve this poison
that brews inside my body?
I promise to be good and wholesome,
please let this torture subside.

If I'm at fault, then I can change,
this control is my powerful charge.
I'll live with what is dealt to me
without guilt or remaining in a fog.

So, horrible disease, please understand
that I'm not that scared of you,
and take your menacing cells away
this body is not going to submit, that's true.

I've lived each day in fear
that I'll be dead by your menacing power,
however I've chosen to live my life
without worry or fear or horror.

Personal Feelings

Did I Deserve This?

I get the impression you feel that I have
had control of these poisonous cells.
I torture myself every day that our lives
have been put into a terrible hell.

I know that I'm not the same person,
you wanted to have in your life.
The disease is so powerful and all consuming
each day that I try to fight.

Did I deserve this powerful enemy
that fills my mind every day?
My thoughts are like a tornado of questions,
that spins out of control, not allowing me time to play.

I didn't deserve this horrible disease
or deserve the scorn I feel.
I'm doing the best that my body can do
to bring back my life with zeal.

Please put yourself inside my shoes
and feel the pain I have,
this malady is part of who I am
so don't look oh so sad.

I didn't deserve this or wish it to be
or want it to hang around,
but this is my new life …
that will be with me forever …
so understand and please stick around.

Personal Feelings

I Am So Afraid

The dark clouds hover,
they make my day so gray,
they follow me everywhere I go,
not allowing me time to play.

Each day I see in front of me,
DEATH that's become an unwanted friend,
it's not the thing I want with me
so I try to ignore and pretend.

I am so afraid my illness will return,
my friends have fallen before.
My mind keeps trying to fool itself,
but the thoughts return that I abhor.

I am so afraid to lose my fight,
I care to live more years.
I'll try to see within the life I've been dealt,
with rainbows and lots of cheers.

I want support, not pity for me,
or sorrow for what might become.
Please hold me tight inside your arms,
this fight, together, can be won.

Personal Feelings

I Cry All Day Long

It doesn't take much to make me cry,
my eyes leak without control.
My head spins with thoughts of death,
it consumes my body and soul.

My emotions are raw like a fresh burn,
that never heals or goes away.
It causes my tears to return again,
not allowing me time for play.

I cry inside with my shell intact,
masking the misery that I feel.
The world sees only a happy face,
while my mind ponders what's quite so real.

One day I'll let go and release all my tears,
if I feel warm and safe with some love.
I'm waiting for the day when I can say,
"I'm all right—my illness is gone."

Please understand that I'm frail at this time,
and in need of support and some care.
It will be a help if you can be by my side
when the thoughts of disease reappear.

Personal Feelings

Where's My Joy?

I used to be such a happy person
dancing as I walked.
Today the music is turned on mute
no passion when I talk.

I blame the disorder, it bullies me,
and takes away my joy.
I wish my happiness would return some day,
instead of anxiety and my scorn.

I battle each day, my fists are raw,
as I pummel the ugly word.
My goal is to find the strength deep inside,
so my joy has a home that can be heard.

Personal Feelings

Is My Attitude Gone?

It's hard at times to roll out of bed,
to even think my future is truly bright.
I wallow in my thoughts that I will die tomorrow,
to plan requires a mighty fight.

My attitude is one of sorrow,
that I've been dealt a raw blow.
I look at myself with self-pity,
just waiting for my time to go.

There was a time when I saw my life,
from rosier, happy eyes.
It's gone away and left me alone …
I stay in bed to hide.

I hear the attitudes of other survivors,
their dreams say they have control.
I am not ready to falsely see,
a positive world that I can't hold.

I want my old attitude to come back to me,
this torture is too hard to bear.
I wish for days of happiness,
pushing out my thoughts of despair.

My community of survivors pushes me toward
a different frame of mind.
It is too hard to remove my fears,
my worries are there all the time.

I know that my attitude needs to change,
if I am to truly survive.
I'll give it a try to remember the days,
when I was happy and knew I was really alive.

Personal Feelings

My Moments Are Like Grains of Sand

The life I have is fragile,
my feelings are gone from me.
I struggle every day with my fear,
wondering what life has in store to see.

I see my life in the palm of my hand,
I used to have a solid base,
but now those feelings are falling apart,
and starting to blow away.

My moments are like grains of sand,
falling one by one to the ground.
They find the cracks inside my mind
and flutter and spin around.

My mind has to re-think who I am today,
and appreciate what life has in store,
and not allow my grains of sand to disappear
from my soul anymore.

Personal Feelings

Afraid of Not Knowing

Each day I awake with fear in my heart,
I feel the pain inside.
I want to be a real survivor
not afraid or wanting to hide.

But I don't know if what I do
will keep me above the ground.
I am afraid of not knowing
how long I'm going to be around.

Remission is a positive word,
it's there to give me hope,
however it has no guarantees,
that it's not really a joke.

I am afraid of not knowing
if my illness will ever return.
I'll go along with enough blind faith,
that survivors hold tight in their hands.

One thing I know is that today I'm alive,
that is a *known* that's just for me.
So I'll just live each day I have,
with wonder, courage, and spirituality.

Personal Feelings

I Want Control Over Something

It is not fair how my life has changed,
or how I move each day.
I want control over something good,
I'm ready to love and play.

Fatigue and worry control my body,
they drain the life from me.
I want to get control of my days,
to enjoy the days I see.

The thoughts of loss, the thoughts of death,
are with me all the time.
They control my moods and energy,
they're so disgustingly intertwined.

I want control today for me,
I want it in my life.
I want to enjoy the passion I used to feel,
and become once again a loving wife.

I ask for patience, understanding too,
my life seems out of control.
Please walk with me hand in hand,
that's all I can hope to hold.

Personal Feelings

Lost Within a Poison

I cannot forgive myself
for being so careless with my life.
I play mind games every moment I can,
wondering if I've caused myself to die.

I'm lost within this emotional poison,
as it crawls around inside.
My mind will not give me a reprieve,
as I struggle to be alive.

Sometimes I just don't want to think
that a future is in store for me.
It is the curse of Cancer,
that just won't let me be.

I'm lost, adrift, alone at times,
no hope or confidence abound.
This poison that is inside of me,
has a power that's so profound.

I need the power, the strength, the hope,
to kill the poison in my mind.
It will take some help from the people I love,
to leave this battle behind.

Personal Feelings

Personal Feelings

Section 2

HANDLING BEING AFRAID

Being afraid is something that is perfectly natural when a devastating illness comes into your life. How do you overcome the daily anxiety, the hopelessness, the isolation, and the inability to cope? How do you hold life in one hand and death in the other?

It requires a horrific balancing act that most of us are not equipped to do. You need to see life as a crapshoot, you are the "house," and the odds are in your favor to win. Will this boastful attitude instantly remove the fear you feel about suffering or dying? It might. Having the right attitude can move mountains.

Writing down your feelings in this interactive journal is a big step toward putting things in your favor and gaining control over the emotional part of the disease.

Before disease or the loss of a loved one entered your life, death was a philosophical topic for discussion. However, it is now a reality and that makes it a whole new point of debate. You can try to see with positive eyes the success stories that surround you, but the reality is, your mind drifts towards a negative attitude that wouldn't wish on your worst enemy.

Is there a lesson from all of this? Yes. You have no control over any of it. The only control you have is to take care of your wellness. You are not responsible for getting your disease or for the loss of a loved one. Dealing with the pain is hard enough; so don't waste your time dealing with a burden you didn't create. Your responsibility is to do everything you can to live a happy and fulfilled life.

Before disease entered your life, did you know how long you had to live? Then why worry about death now? Live life as if today was your last. Right now is your best opportunity to taste the world that has escaped you for so long.

As you continue to write, journey with the goal of putting your words and honesty out there, so you can discover that the transference of your thoughts, anxieties, worries, and fears onto paper will delegate your disease mind-set to rest. You need to give your brain a rest, as it swells, expanding your thoughts in such a manner that begins to harm your health. You worry. You lose sleep. You even neglect yourself.

To remove the emotions of being afraid, you must understand yourself honestly. The next series of poems were written to help you deal and cope with fears so you can begin to see the new, wonderful horizons that are waiting to be explored.

Live in the moment and enjoy it. Moments will become days, then weeks, then months, and finally years, making what time you have left an experience to remember. A Mind Diet.

Exercise

List ten things you feel you have lost since this disease or loss entered your life.

1.
2.
3.
4.
5.
6.
7.
8.
9.
10.

Every Pain Scares Me

I take a breath, my food of life,
something different comes over me.
My mind begins to feel a pain,
its origin is hard to see.

I worry that it's back again,
my brain is on overload.
How can I keep doing this dance,
and putting my life on hold?

I feel my breasts, my insides too,
the pain seems oh so real.
I worry every second I have,
I thought I was ready to heal.

Each day I balance life and death,
my scale tips toward death each time.
I struggle hard to tip the scale
so life will begin to chime.

My mind is not a friend at times,
it plays a nasty game.
It likes to twist my thoughts around,
draining my energy and placing blame.

Is there a lesson from all of this?
Or is my life on hold?
I have to find the control I need,
so my body won't collapse and fold.

Personal Feelings

No Beginnings

I am a survivor, that fact is true,
it is a label placed on me.
My future is supposed to become
as bright as it can be.

But where is a beginning?
I don't feel there is an end.
Do I really have a tomorrow
to share with all my friends?

I've stopped planning or looking toward,
future pleasures that lurk around.
I have no beginnings to grab on to,
my life seems upside down.

What if I try to begin something new,
and then tomorrow I'm gone?
I am bewildered just where to start
so I can finally be able to move on.

I see no beginnings to my life today,
or ways to start anew.
I feel so trapped inside my thoughts,
my life seems very blue.

What if I blindly begin to see,
a future down the road?
Will I have extra tomorrows for me,
to treasure and to hold?

What can I lose if I try to walk
into my terrible storm?
It might just let me pop on out,
and find a beginning so I can be strong.

Personal Feelings

Leave Me My Dreams

I once had dreams that filled my head.
I once had thoughts that were wild.
I wish I could go back and become,
that innocent, playful child.

My dreams were real and filled with hope,
of a future that allowed me in.
But now I have let all my dreams evaporate,
blown away by a murderous wind.

I search each day with energy lost,
with fatigue that drags me down.
My dreams are gone, they've floated away,
to a place I don't want to belong.

I have to understand that life for me
is not what it once had been.
It has a new direction,
that hit me on my chin.

So what if all my old dreams are lost,
or have simply faded away?
I am a new person who sees her life,
that can have new dreams to help form a new way.

I'll make my dreams fit my new life,
the change will do me good.
My dreams are something that come from the heart,
I'm glad it is finally understood.

Personal Feelings

New Friends

I've gained a community
that previously was unknown,
their support shines on me clear.
They are my new friends that share my pain,
standing by me as I shed my tears.

The friends I still know,
from a past I can't see,
seem confused and unable to help.
They see the death that surrounds my disease,
avoiding the right words to help me cope.

I've changed and I've grown
with a power so strong,
but my friends seem to have drifted far away.
Until they can see the new person in me,
I will survive as I move on my way.

The life that I knew is gone from me now,
along with how I saw friends once before.
My outlook will be one of open honesty
with my arms open wide at my door.

So all I ask is that all of my friends
just bask in the new pleasures I now adore.
And see me with eyes that have love deep inside
because I'm going to be around forevermore.

Personal Feelings

Ding Dong, The Disease is All Gone

I struggle each day,
my mind is in knots,
I worry if my illness is near.
I wish I could ring a loud bell every hour
signaling to all, my disease has disappeared.

It must be a joke that I feel oh so well,
when I'm told that there is no cure.
It's hard moving on
with these thoughts of despair,
and the hope that is just all in my mind.

I laugh and I cry,
but the reality won't subside, as it
slaps me hard inside my heart.
But I try because I must
or my brain will just expand and bust
as this illness keeps staying so near.

The worry that I can't bear
is the thought of the fear,
of my independence being taken away.
So I pull at the rope with all the strength and the hope
that my disease will never again come near.

"Ding dong, my disease is all gone,"
is the chant I say inside my head.
I'll ring that damn bell
until my ill thoughts go to hell
and my life will once again appear.

Personal Feelings

Bucket of Tears

I never know when the tears will come,
my fear just enters and goes.
I try so hard to hide my pain
but my bucket of tears always shows.

This body I have is really not mine,
my life is like a horrible dream.
I shiver and shake at the thoughts in my head
that continue to make my heart want to scream.

It is not fair to go on each day
with answers that seem so vague.
But the people I trust with my care
can't stop my mind that aches.

I cry each day a bucket of tears,
I just can't control my emotions.
The people around me shudder and shake
misunderstanding my fear and confusion.

I have to be firm, be in control,
or fear will continue to take over my life.
It's me who has the power to try,
to dictate how well I'll be able to fight.

I will be strong, even on my own,
I'll move with grace and dignity.
And when I cry my bucket of tears
it will be from my greatest victory.

Personal Feelings

I Don't Feel Passion

My passion has been replaced with an energy
that is focused only on me.
The life I once had has been put on hold,
as I struggle to try to be free.

It's not that I don't feel so in love,
or have the need for tender warmth.
It's just that I am in a fight for my life
that keeps me drained, not seeing my worth.

I wish it all could be put aside
and my life once again be like new.
But I have a cancer that has a terrible passion
that's trying to take me from you.

Right now I don't feel the energy to plan
a future without this disease.
However, I still love you just the same,
just with less energy and much grief.

I am very afraid to put my thoughts on hold
and forget that death has arrived.
I'm convinced my mind can defeat
this disease if only I continue to try.

Please don't confuse my lack of passion
for a lack of love for you.
I need you more than ever to help,
this fight is also for you.

Personal Feelings

Will I Ever Want Sex Again?

I want to feel sexual again,
I want you to touch me with care.
I want to feel you hug me tight
as I shed my painful tears.

I might not feel like making the first move,
it's not a reflection on you.
To fight for my life every day,
keeps consuming my amorous moods.

Don't read into the moods you see,
that sex is gone for good.
I just have other things I'm thinking about,
I hope it's understood.

Please come to me with love in your eyes,
I want you oh so much.
I just require that you try at first
to be soft as you begin to touch.

My body has changed, along with my mind,
my physical appearance might not be the same.
I'm still the woman you once loved with your heart,
please be willing to explore new ways.

We will have sex. I want it so.
I want to feel your love.
Just please be patient with my moods,
my struggle is really hard.

Personal Feelings

I Can't Make It Right

The doctors shrug their shoulders,
they have no answers to give,
they only know I have a death sentence
that will come, that's understood.

I cannot find the answers
to make my life again right.
It's hard to wage a battle
or to even try to fight.

I want to make everything all right,
I try to see things so bright.
I try to go each day I'm alive
ignoring what's in my sights.

I cry each day, there's no power in me,
my body is drained by fear.
Why can't I make everything all right,
to increase my remaining years?

I blame myself for what's happened to me,
I bathe inside my sorrow.
I wish that I could just fix it now
and not worry about my tomorrows.

Each day I'll go in a forward way,
knowing I cannot make this cancer right.
But that won't stop me from being strong
and putting up a good fight.

Personal Feelings

Can You Watch Me Die?

I add to all my worries,
just how you'll cope and be.
I wonder how you'll deal
when death comes over me.

Can you watch me die?
Or can you stand real strong?
I fear that when the time has come,
you'll be destroyed after I move along.

I am not afraid of facing death
It's been a part of me.
I just can't picture how you'll act
when death wins out while you see.

Can you really watch me die?
Or will you crumble and fall?
I want you to know I've loved my life,
especially our years most of all.

Don't weep for me,
but bring to your mind,
the time we've had until now,
and remember the times we've spent together
without consuming all your sorrows.

Please watch me die
and hold me tight
and feel the last life drain from me
and try to love the ending you see,
it's our last experience that was meant to be.

Our love has come full circle,
I'm sorry I have to leave,
just watch me die and if you cry
I'll take your tears with me.

Personal Feelings

Personal Feelings

Section 3

Afraid to Lose My Independence

One of the biggest concerns most cancer patients have is not being able to live life under their own terms. They fear that their new boss (Cancer) will become ruthless, removing their ability to care for themselves. One cancer patient I interviewed told me, *"I fear that I won't be able to care for myself and it will force me to give up the life that I want."* Another survivor said, *"I don't want to lose my beautiful hair. Wearing wigs is just not me."*

How can cancer take away your independence? You can lose the power to propel yourself forward, the human connection becomes strained, you stop believing, you focus on the negative, you turn away from support, you surrender to you're the disease, you forget to forgive, and you take away any chances of finding joy in your life.

As your body begins to change and fatigue increases, your

mind starts to dwell on harmful things. Anger sets in, you focus on the pain, and then your mind takes over with a hurricane of worries, anxieties, and uncertainties, until you are paralyzed and unable to deal with your diseased life. Instead of being independent, you have become dependent.

Cancer can be a temporary interruption or it can cause drastic life changes. Either way, cancer will move at supersonic speed to take away your independence. The beginning of treatment can be the most devastating time on your outlook of the future. The fatigue, the constant retching of your guts, the loss of hair, and not being able to take care of yourself like you once did, can wreak havoc on your mental ability to cope.

Once you lose your ability to cope, your independence flies out the window. I've been told that some people experience a heavy fog that surrounds them and hides any chance to find the right direction to take in the recovery process. They surround themselves with support groups, but the ugly thoughts lay stagnant inside their heads.

Another factor that comes into the picture is the loneliness cancer patients feel during their treatments. Being isolated in one's mind, when concrete answers about recovery and the future are not available, can drain what little resolve and independence you have.

Will your independence return? Yes. When? No one can tell you. It is an individual thing that will get magnified as you go through your treatments. How you dealt with difficult situations in the past will be an example of how you'll deal with the most devastating situation of your life.

The next series of poems should stir up hidden feelings that can help you find the independence you'll need to succeed and to have a productive future. Cancer might just be your wake-up call to start your life over. Experiencing death puts a whole new slant of life. You begin to finally understand that you only have so much time to live and to do the things you really want to do.

Don't wait until it is too late and you're sitting in your rocking chair or on your deathbed, wishing you had more time. You have the time now, even if it is a month, a year, or a lifetime. Take command of yourself and don't allow the disease to slow you down.

Too many cancer patients turn inside themselves, hiding from the world the painful secret that they have cancer. Hiding the truth from people in your life, especially those you love, can be the most effective way of losing your independence. Openness allows you to go through many important doors on your way to recovery.

Use your poems to find the hidden truths inside your minds. Listen to them, trust them, and they will become your best friends. Only you can take away your independence and only you can control how your cancer will affect every aspect of your life.

This is the time when you need to show support for your wife as she tries to change and find new independence. Don't be afraid that you are losing her, instead see it as a wonderful opportunity to discover a new and beautiful friend in your life.

Exercise

As a couple make a list of all the things that have changed in your lives since cancer became a guest. This list should include everything both of you feel is gone from your lives and that you wish could be returned:

1.
2.
3.
4.
5.
6.
7.
8.
9.
10.

Now make a list of all the things that are in your lives that cancer created and that you wish were not around:

1.
2.
3.
4.
5.
6.
7.
8.
9.
10.

Out of Control

I feel surrounded
consumed with fear,
my body is failing me now.
I can't see straight
or think quite clear,
my energy is lost somewhere.

Sometimes I'm rational,
other times I'm clear,
then my body rebels on me.
I twist and turn,
I cry at times,
my mind is riddled with fear.

I can't control what flows through me,
or stop my ghastly thoughts.
I am so terribly out of control,
my thinking is the worst.

I cannot focus or concentrate,
my thoughts are really not mine.
It is the cancer that's controlling me,
my future seems hard to find.

The unknown just hovers over me,
the clouds are dark and gray.
I hate to be empowered by
this torture that wants to play.

I pray one day to get back my control
and push out all of my fears,
and tell this cancer that I'm the boss
every day, every month, and every year.

Personal Feelings

I See Death All Around Me

Sometimes I feel joy
surround my body and my soul,
but then my mind slips into a dark place
breaking my resolve.

It's death that comes knocking
at my private door of life.
It hits me hard with the truth that lurks,
beneath my callous hide.

Another friend has succumbed
to the cancer that's inside of me,
and brings to life that my future hasn't changed
or that my remission will stay with me.

My community of support is just like me,
with fears that hide inside.
This occasion of death has missed us all,
letting us know our time can't hide.

I want to keep my positive moods,
and live my life each day,
I just wish that death would not be around
to remind me what's at stake.

I can rationalize that those survivors made
a good fight and did the best they could,
but knowing that my death could come,
cannot be understood.

I know that death is all around,
it's the curse that came to me,
I'll try to let it hover above
before it smothers me.

Personal Feelings

Too Many Healthy People Near Me

They go through life without a care,
they abuse their bodies and soul,
they are so blind to what life is about,
they laugh when they are told.

They flaunt their careless attitude,
they prance with eyes so blind.
I hate them all
that they can't see
that life has precious time.

I struggle with life,
with eyes quite wide,
it stares at me all day.
I'm jealous that I have one choice,
to survive for another day.

I try to laugh deep inside my heart
and enjoy the life I have,
but the healthy people that I see,
remind me of a life that left me sad.

I'll try to become healthy and free,
if only inside my mind,
and let my cancer do what it needs to do,
as I enjoy my remaining time.

Personal Feelings

Horrible Messages

Am I disfigured, or pretty to see?
That question lies inside my head.
The way I walk and dress for life,
should be the happiest part, not dread.

But I see your stares,
and pathetic eyes,
that try to hide the pity that they feel.
It hurts my heart to know that you
are not comfortable with what is now real.

These are horrible messages
that pierce my heart,
your face is like an open book.
I wish that you could see just me,
and not the way I look.

I want you to see
that I still have beauty,
even though my cancer has struck.
I am alive with hope and pride,
never wanting to give up.

You have a choice to look inside
and go through my carved up shell,
and see the person deep inside
who needs love to make her well.

I have a legacy that includes pain
that will always be in my heart,
I need the message that you still care,
so our life won't fall apart.

Believe in the here-and-now,
and not what might have been,
and keep the horrible messages away,
so our new life has a place to begin.

Personal Feelings

How Strong Can I Be?

Will my life be carved by me?
Or will the cancer consume?
Will I venture out today?
Or stay inside my room?

Should I share my desperate needs?
Or simply go alone?
I just worry all day long,
If I can be very strong.

So my life is not the same,
it's said that change is good.
Will I have the energy to try
to continue and resume?

I don't want to appear too weak,
or fail to stand real tall.
I am afraid that someone will take
my independence as I fall.

I need someone to stand by me,
to steady me as I go.
I need that support for just awhile
to get strong so you can go.

When I feel strong
I'll come back in style,
with ribbons that flow on the wind.
And show you just how strong I am
and that I'm going to win.

Patience is something we need to share,
to move on down the road.
With little steps
we'll achieve our goal
and be strong with a life that's not on hold.

Personal Feelings

Needy Schmeedy

Most days I sulk within myself,
it's hard to move about.
I struggle with life's only question:
When will death finally come about?

I feel quite silly,
so dependent on support,
afraid to ask for help this day,
I feel so very distraught with worry
hoping my cancer will go away.

I see myself as needy schmeedy,
my thoughts are out of sync.
I want to not give into my fears,
but I feel as if I'll sink.

Please hold me tight and squeeze away
the terror that comes and goes,
and press it very hard with your arms,
and push it out through my toes.

My apparent needs are not a sign
that I'm completely out of whack,
it's just one of those crazy thoughts
that keeps on coming back.

I am still strong,
I work real hard
to keep myself in shape.
It's just that sometimes
I overload and feel like I'm going to break.

Please accept my needy schmeedy ways
and understand my pain.
This death that floats above my head
is like a heavy rain.

It's temporary, I promise you this.
So face me with your smile,
and support me with your loving arms
as I struggle for awhile.

Personal Feelings

Personal Feelings

Too Much Caring

I hate to complain, my problems are mine,
everyone around me looks so sad.
I feel that too much caring for me
reminds me of the horror inside my head.

At times I try to keep my pain,
hidden deep inside my mind,
so I can go a day alone,
to deal and not feel so entwined.

I have my worries, my fear of death
and leaving all my friends behind.
But too much caring is not helping now,
as I work toward this cure of mine.

All I need is a strong tree to lean on,
with silence and strength near me,
this is my wish for all the love
that keeps dripping all over me.

Personal Feelings

Let Me Find My Own Way

We're in this together; our goals are the same,
the struggle is ours to bear.
But I need to figure things out alone,
away from our love, before it tears.

Let me find my own way,
it is how I'll conquer the cancer I have,
and be understanding during this time we're alone
and don't let my actions make you sad.

I will always return during our day
and give you as much love as I can,
with patience and hope that we both need to show
it will let me deal with my disease that's at hand.

Personal Feelings

I Don't Want to Feel so Tired

My body that was once my friend
has deserted me and left me alone.
I trusted that I could be strong and a fighter
as my disease kept singing its song.

I've never known such fatigue like this,
it affects my mind so I can't think.
My body responds with a strange, uncanny weakness,
that won't let me work or be in the pink.

I struggle each day with the hope that I'll find
a way to get out of bed,
and find that part of me that once ran around
with a smile and not feeling so sad.

I don't want to feel so tired
or not be there for the people I love.
I want to again be able to nurture
and get back to the life I once had.

But my recovery zaps the energy from me,
which continues to keep me so sad.
So please understand my fatigue is not directed at you,
I just don't want you becoming too mad.

Personal Feelings

Personal Feelings

Section 4

LACK OF TRUST

When I first found out I had heart disease I thought the doctors were referring to someone else. I remember when my wife, Nancy, was diagnosed with breast cancer; I believed someone had made a big mistake. It is sometimes hard to trust the professionals that want to cure your illness because they remain emotionally aloof as you struggle to emotionally survive.

How do you trust the people in your life with your personal weakness—the realization that you are not immortal—and show them how scared you are? When heart disease entered my life, I wanted to deal with it on my own, emotionally that is. I did not want to admit that I was not the invincible man who stared back at me in the mirror every day.

Exposing a physical weakness can jeopardize a career, disrupt a relationship, and even cause chronic depression. How do you learn to trust yourself and the people that float in and out of your life on a daily basis? The first step is to learn to communicate honestly. This might be harder for you than dealing with your illness.

The next step is to put your thoughts, fears, and anxieties on paper. Getting those horrible emotions out of your head in written form, hopefully in a creative manner, will open up a part of you that will provide many needed answers, so you can learn to trust yourself and the world around you.

Why have I written a book for couples that are dealing with a life-threatening illness? Relationships, even those based on love and trust, can become strained as one of the partners struggles to recover from an illness. It is important that each member of the team learns to stay open with his or her communication.

Watching a wonderful relationship, the partnership that you believed would never change, come to a drastic halt, can create an emotional shock. This change in your life needs to be dealt with properly or it can seriously affect your future.

As a man I believed that all problems could be solved logically. I practiced that philosophy during my thirty-five years of working within the business community. Having a life-threatening disease consume me, instilled a lot of empathy for others inflicted with an illness, especially when it was the one person in my life who I loved more than life itself. I will not accept as true that if I hadn't gotten heart disease my support and understanding for Nancy would have been different.

However, statistics show that there is a higher percentage of women with breast cancer being divorced by their husbands than those with any other form of cancer.

I have often wondered how a spouse could turn his or her back on someone they love when a life-threatening illness affects their relationship. Was the relationship flawed before the disease came knocking? Was the relationship lacking good communication skills? Was the relationship unilateral, where the woman was the family caregiver and nurturer? It might be a combination of all of these things; nevertheless, I believe trust is the real issue.

This section is dedicated to re-learning how to trust each other and build a new and stronger bond in your relationship. Couples have to realize that many things they had taken for granted in their relationship before disease moved into their lives, will be changed or readjusted. You will never go back to the place you had before disease moved into your home.

Learning to trust yourself first will make trusting your partner easier. It can be very easy to avoid communicating. In most cases, the patient tries to hide the truth from a spouse or significant other with the hope of not being a burden. I have done this many times, like hiding from my wife when I needed to pop a nitroglycerin tablet under my tongue. A crazy year of going in and out of hospitals, having numerous operations, and ultimately a quadruple bypass, was shocking to my wife, because I had pretended I was all right.

My logic seemed reasonable at the time. Nancy was still struggling with her own recovery from breast cancer and did not need any additional stress. I finally realized that my logic was flawed, however, since she worried about me MORE because she did not trust I wasn't going to drop dead of a heart attack one day.

I now trust that she is stronger than I had originally thought and I keep her abreast of my health. The ability to communicate my fears and anxieties has made us closer. Trusting our relationship with our mortality has made us even stronger. We communicate verbally and through journaling. While the relationship we once had, pre-heart disease and pre-breast cancer, is not the same, our marriage has grown to a new and more passionate level than I had ever imagined.

Today, I still live with chest pains that need to be controlled through stress reduction, medication, and the will power to make my heart disease improve. I have learned to be a different type of caregiver and nurturer to the woman I love. I like who I have become. It has brought a new dimension to our marriage. I have learned to embrace the changes that come into my life every day and I want to help you discover how to trust yourself and the people in your life that matter the most to you.

Can someone with a life-threatening illness learn to trust life and try to live every day like there is no tomorrow? Yes. For me it has been through my writing and not allowing my chest pains to control me. Can this attitude work for someone with cancer? I believe so. I've witnessed my wife, a cancer survivor, use her artistic skills and writing to allow her to live in the todays of her life.

Does she worry about her cancer returning? I know for a fact that she does, however she does not allow her thoughts to interrupt the important things she wants to do in her life. She has taught me over the years that you cannot have any tomorrows without todays—and that is exactly what I hope this chapter will imprint on you.

Can we trust our own bodies again? Can we look at our loved one with eyes that do not bring fear into our soul? The answer for me is no. But, as the husband of a cancer survivor and a man with heart disease, I can honestly say I am living today with no regrets and looking forward to as many tomorrows as I can possibly have.

I am currently writing a novel called *Waiting For Tomorrow*. It is about a man who waited too long to make amends with his two best friends before they died. he idea came to me after I lost nine friends and family members in a ten-month period. The message here is that I am learning to trust life and see it for what it truly is: a wonderful piece of art that needs to be appreciated and treasured every day.

Do not allow your pain, fears, anxieties, worries, sorrows, and thoughts about mortality to consume you. Death will happen one day, that is a fact. However, if you live each day like there is no tomorrow, not recklessly, but with passion for yourself and the people in your life that you love, you will end your journey one day with no regrets.

Do not wait for tomorrow to do the things you have always wanted to do. Don't let your physical limitations hinder your ability to find pleasure in your life. Do not give up on yourself or your partner. Learn to trust and enjoy the life you have been dealt.

Hopeless Thoughts

I know the strength that's inside of me
as I struggle with recovery every day,
but I can't seem to shake a feeling
that I'm alone because I can't play.

I have these hopeless thoughts each day
that death will find me alone
and take the breath that's inside of me
to a place I don't belong.

I have around me my helpful friends,
my spouse who tries his best,
but I can't rid my mind of the pain
my hopeless feelings get.

What can I say or can I do
to be stronger than I am?
I'm afraid to ask for too much help
as I struggle as hard as I can.

Personal Feelings

Another Friend Has Died

It's not supposed to happen
that death still follows me,
but its smell fills my nostrils
with a blanket of fear that only I can see.

Its stench comes floating by
and plants itself within my soul
and makes me want to scream and cry
it's such a living hell.

I've done my best, just like my friends,
the sisters of cancer that support,
but they are falling fast away,
the loneliness continues to hurt.

I hate to read the letters and
the e-mails and take the phone calls,
but what I hate the most each day
is knowing I could possibly fall.

I must admit I'm scared as hell,
that my battle will defeat and maim
and that the pleasures we seek for our future
will vanish due to the cancer game.

If I believe that death is there,
that friends will fall like rain,
I'll try to hold my umbrella real close
so the raindrops won't do me the same.

Personal Feelings

Am I Next?

I have a reality, that death is on its way
and I am not immortal as once I thought,
but am I next? I do not know
as I walk and waddle along.

I will not guess or try to predict
the time that's left for me,
I have enough seconds left to see
fulfilled and happy as I can be.

So if I'm next, well bring it on,
I won't quit without a fight,
I've been told before that I will die
yet won that nasty fight.

I've learned to accept fear each day,
to accept that my time is short,
but understand that the time that I'm here
I'll be happy with no regrets.

Personal Feelings

Endless Struggles

I feel a pain, my mind torments,
I crumble that my cancer has returned.
I feel so tired of these endless struggles,
it's a place I don't want to belong.

I understand that I'm supposed to be positive,
it's a part of the healing process,
but I can't stop thinking of the endless struggles
that are tearing me apart.

I'm not really sure if I could fight as hard
as I did a while ago,
the torment that I feel that it could start all over
is the struggle I don't want to know.

These endless struggles never go away
or leave me while I sleep.
I need to feel a peace over me
to consume what my mind really believes.

Please look at me and see my plight,
the concern that blankets my fragile soul
and hold me tight during these endless struggles,
I don't want to go through them alone.

Personal Feelings

It's Not Fair

My thoughts don't trust,
my feelings are frail,
my life seems out of control,
I have a cancer that is stuck inside,
never easing or leaving me alone.

It's just not fair to carry this weight
or to not be the person I once was.
I see in your eyes the fear that you carry
that tomorrow I might not be around.

It is not fair, the torture, this cancer
keeps affecting my life each day,
it might be gone as I try to carry on
but it lingers.
It's just not fair.

Please hold me close and whisper to me
that my frailty will not change our love
and tell me your thoughts
of how unfair this all feels,
it's the words that will fit like a glove.

Personal Feelings

I See The Pain in Your Eyes

Together we feel,
together we love,
together we share pain,
it beams from our eyes
with a sadness that's no surprise
as we wait during this cancer game.

I see your pain,
it fills your eyes
and washes over me with a rush.
I struggle inside seeing the pain in your eyes,
I am sorry I can't do enough.

I see the pain
and still love you so
and wish I could make things seem okay,
but I know that what's inside
wants to be silent and hide
and not face the truth that we feel every day.

I see the pain that's in your eyes
and will smile and hug you tight
and promise that my fear will be spoken
so you can hear everything will be all right.

Personal Feelings

Is There A Future For Me?

I once had dreams to live a life without worry,
filled with peace and tranquility.
But now I'm sick and those dreams have changed
putting me in a state of immobility.

What has the future in store for me?
What can I expect?
How can I think of my loving plans
when I feel so darn upset?

Will tomorrow really come?
Or will I just sit and wait?
It wasn't what I planned to do
but I can't overcome this heartache.

Is there a future for me that I will love?
Can I see colors once more?
I still hear inside my head
the cancer message louder than before.

I need a push, maybe a little help,
something to make me believe,
but most of all inside my mind
is that I'm just not ready to leave.

Cancer is my future?
The choice was taken from me,
but I will try to see each day
as happy as I can be.

Today I'll plant my feet
and trust that they will move on,
toward a place that's colorful and tranquil
it's the place I want to belong.

Personal Feelings

Can I Laugh?

I force myself to smile each day,
to find a happy place,
but will I ever truly laugh again?
It seems like such a distant place.

I feel the laughter inside my soul,
it waits for a time that is not there,
it waits with patience, wanting to surface
but is blanketed by my despair.

I want to laugh, to feel the joy
that once gave freedom to me.
I need to see the fun in my life
that this cancer prevents me to see.

Maybe I'll find some joy inside,
some funny things about my plight.
I'll look at all the weird things that have happened lately
and laugh with firm delight.

Can I laugh?
Oh, yes I can
with the joke this life's passed on to me
and look this cancer in the eye
laughing as hard as I want the world to see.

Personal Feelings

What Can I Do?

I hear this question every day
it swirls inside my head.
It comes from people close and caring,
helpless as they can be.

I don't know how to answer myself
or answer those caring souls.
I feel a lack of trust with life
that's put me on a horrible hold.

This answer is a difficult one,
it changes each day with my moods.
If I don't understand it myself,
how can I make myself understood?

There is nothing anyone can do
to cure my cancer thoughts,
they just have to understand that each day
my mind is like a fort.

I do resist letting my disease
take over and get me down.
That's what I can do to help myself
and remove this sadness frown.

Personal Feelings

Emotionally Drained

To think the cancer inside of me
every moment of my day,
just drains the living hell from me
as I try to move and play.

I am so emotionally drained at times,
when I allow myself to think,
my thoughts go straight to death each time
as my life seems confused and weak.

It's not too easy to change your thoughts
or keep death away from your door,
but I'll commit to finding some thoughts
that won't drain me anymore.

I will at times be emotionally drained
and at times be filled with energy abound,
but please don't think each day will be like before,
I still have my cancer around.

Personal Feelings

Personal Feelings

Section 5

Is Death in My Future?

How should you ponder the question of when someone will die? When struck with a disease that is incurable, but might remain dormant for years, this question can be unbearable.

Do you think about death and the possibility that cancer will rear its ugly head again? Should you become your own cheerleader and move forward, defying the disease as if it never existed?

Some would say that is a healthy approach. Keeping your emotions positive can only help during recovery. Unfortunately our minds don't really bury our thoughts when we act positive and enthusiastic. Like cancer, these thoughts remain in a black hole inside our heads, coming out to play when we are alone in a private, quiet place.

I believe you should think about death and the cancer that might be hiding, and face it head-on. Become the manager of your thoughts and, like all good managers, delegate the problem to someone or something else: your rhythm poem journal.

Make up as many crazy, funny, sad, and bewildering titles of your emotions and write with honesty and truth about how you feel at that moment. Death is in all of our futures, but you don't have to sit down like a couch potato, vegetating until it happens.

You need to express yourself and let your words sing on the pages, loudly so that you and the world can hear and understand the truth about how you are choosing to fight this horrible disease. It is not just the survivor who has to sing the painful thoughts, but also the spouse who is feeling the same pain and sorrow.

Exercise

Take a moment and write down all the fear, tension, and depression that you are feeling at this time. Try to write at least ten and then make up titles for each of the emotions you've written down. Then share them with your partner and write down what your spouse has told you.

1.
2.
3.
4.
5.
6.
7.
8.
9.
10.

As you read the poems in this chapter you will have a better feeling for what needs to be said, first to yourself and then to your spouse. Death should not be a frightening event, but rather a period of your life that will someday have to be confronted. Why not begin dealing with the here and now, while you're alive and active? It will be harder and more painful the longer you wait.

Can I Battle Death?

Today I awake and know I'm alive,
the clock begins to tick.
My mind begins its daily routine
to tell my body not to quit.

What quality will I have today,
will fatigue consume before I start?
Or will it be the constant worry
that sometimes makes me fall apart?

I force a smile, it appears so real,
but my soul cannot abide,
that like each day that I am alive,
I battle to survive.

There's nothing natural about how I feel
it's a struggle that is my daily routine,
I expel my energy with all my might
to battle these emotions that I feel.

Can I battle death each day?
Can I find some time with peace?
The answers have no solution for me,
as I pray for some needed relief.

My mind has become a tortuous foe,
with many feelings that come and go.
But one that keeps repeating itself
is when will my time melt like spring snow?

Can I battle death each day?
It's a joke that makes me laugh.
Because I have no control over my disease,
as it waits to make me crash.

Personal Feelings

My Eternal Flame

My heart pounds, my mind thinks,
my soul is a fire every day.
That is my eternal flame
that is with me and always is at play.

Cancer is a burning word,
it's a brand that won't ever go away,
its flame is eternal with pending consequences
that keep my old life at bay.

I know that death is following me,
like it follows all of its prey.
I just want some time to live a day
not like a victim with abnormal ways.

My eternal flame is going to
always burn very bright.
It will continue to feel warm and hot,
every morning, noon, and night.

But what I'll try to put in my mind
is a symbol that will be my beacon,
that shows me I still have some fight,
without becoming weakened.

Personal Feelings

My Terms

I have a life, even though I see,
that cancer is now a part of me.
However, I will deal each day I have,
with the energy that is either good or bad.

These are my terms,
I will not stray or falter
as each day comes to an end,
and keep my feelings understanding who I am
as I recover to the new person within my plans.

I have no choice, this life I've been dealt,
but I can choose to do it as I please
and look this cancer in the face
as I battle this nasty disease.

I will choose my terms each day I awake,
unsure of how my body will be,
but reassured today will become
based on the terms that are best for me.

Personal Feelings

Precious Moments

Each day is special and unique for me,
my days are savored with hope.
I understand that this time I have
is no longer a casual joke.

I try to take all my moments
and treasure them with eyes open wide
and know these are my precious moments
that I have while I am still alive.

Some days my thoughts consume my body,
they drag me to the ground,
they pound the energy from my soul
to where I forget why I'm around.

I have to find all my precious moments
and keep them packaged by my side
and let the world know how much I appreciate
that today I'm still alive.

Personal Feelings

Giving Death the Bird

My mother taught me to be respectful,
to treat everything with love and care,
but I just can't bring myself around to appreciate
the cancer that's lurking out there.

Oh God, forgive me for what I might do,
please look the other way.
I have to flip the bird to cancer
with the hope it will go away.

I get so angry as the thoughts creep in
and remind me that a violation of my body exists
and I just can't keep looking the other way
as my thoughts of cancer give me the fits.

I'll turn up my nose, keep my chin held high
and walk with a bounce in my step
and then I'll turn and give death the bird
with a look it will never forget.

So think of me rude or think of me bad
or think my attitude is out of sync,
but understand I'll give you the bird
if you don't think my cancer stinks.

Personal Feelings

Why No Cure?

I raise the funds, I do as I'm told,
I pray every day to my God,
so why is the world unable to find a cure
for the cancer I have?

It's been around for a long, long time,
It's had its reign of death.
So why can't our world find a cure for me
before I'm a casualty that my family won't forget?

I've been so frustrated, so damned depressed,
so unable to sleep at night,
so why can't there be a cure for me
as I battle this nasty fight?

There are no answers. I know that for sure.
To expect one would be absurd.
But can't the smart ones get a little closer
so my day will feel a little more assured?

Why no cure? I do not know.
Nor will I drive myself insane.
I'll just live my life with the hope,
that one day it will all go away.

Personal Feelings

Blue Skies Some Days

Optimism flows through my veins,
I see a future that's there for me.
The skies seem deep and very blue,
as a happiness blankets over me.

I take this joy for what it's worth,
each day is precious and pure.
But experience has taught me well, this feeling
won't last for long.

It can happen like a lightning bolt
or a thought that creeps into my head.
My cancer has no respect for me
as my blue skies begin to fade.

I force a smile. I try to appear,
as strong as I can be.
But the blue skies that I want around,
can turn black as my cancer troubles me.

I fight at times with blame and anger,
I beat myself to death,
that I should try just a little harder
to give my horrid thoughts a rest.

These are my moods,
they trample and pound,
away at my resolve,
but I'll keep looking for my blue skies
every day that I'm around.

Personal Feelings

I Am Rich

I measure my life, this cancerous one
with the people I see each day,
and appreciate the love and concern
that is sent to me in some way.

I am so rich, I am so proud,
that my life has friends who care.
It makes me warm with fuzzy feelings
as I hear their words and prayers.

Each day I'll reflect and count my treasures
and sleep with hope inside,
that all the riches that were with me yesterday
will never ever subside.

So if at times I seem real down,
or consumed and out of sorts,
it's not directed at you at all,
but at my unpleasant, cancerous thoughts.

I am rich with all my friends
who support my spirit and soul,
and will continue to fight each day
to be with you as I get old.

Personal Feelings

Yes, I Will Die

It is a thought that I have each day,
It's with me when I'm with you
that I will die someday,
but I hope it won't be too soon.

Yes, I will die, just like you will some day,
a crystal ball I don't have.
But all I want the days I'm around
is support for the life we have.

I know it's not the same as before
or exactly what you'd like,
but I did not put cancer in my body
to cause our life this strife.

So understand we'll all die someday,
maybe I'll be the one to go first.
But let's take every moment we have
to enjoy our relationship's worth.

Please talk to me about the death in your head,
don't keep it away and locked up.
I want to share your scariest feeling
so we can move forward and not go back.

Please be brave, I know I am.
And please remember our precious love
and treasure the time we have left together
it's a gift that should not be dissolved.

Personal Feelings

Remember Me Today

I've had my years with health and pride
and now it has been taken away.
My body is not what it once was
since this disease came into my life yesterday.

I'm not the same or will ever be,
this curse has changed me so,
but I still have my self-esteem
even if I can't make it show.

My life is what it is today,
I'm a new package for the world to see.
So please when you look deep into my eyes
try to remember the person I used to be.

My future may look dismal,
and not too very clear,
with uncertainty behind every door,
as you try to comfort me.

I need some help to push me toward
the new future that waits each day for me,
so please keep a positive mood
and remember the life that once had been.

Remember me today
and watch me take little steps,
and see the progress that I'll have,
as I fight to be my best.

Personal Feelings

Personal Feelings

Section 6

Living My Dreams

Can you still have dreams after a diagnosis of cancer? Would those dreams turn into nightmares? If you are honest with yourself, your dreams will probably become quite disturbing.

This chapter focuses on how to be honest with the negative thoughts and changes that pop into your head, even when you want to feel positive. Now is the time to find understanding and compassion for this disease. It has become a part of you and remains inside your head. You need to take the bull by the horns and learn how to clear your mind.

You might call this a "mental enema," removing the entire emotional blockage that has built up. When you are done, it will be a true Mind Diet. Everything you've done up to this point has been to help you face the demons that continue to swim inside your thoughts.

Facing the amount of changes that are thrown at the marriage/relationship on a daily basis will increase the stress levels for both partners. If the build-up of stress goes unchecked, your immune systems could become at risk. The survivor can have a relapse and the spouse can develop an illness. This happened to me during my wife's recovery, when I got heart disease. I cannot tell you when my heart disease happened, but I do agree with my doctors that stress played a major role.

Have you ever wondered about that little voice inside your head, the one that speaks to you and tries to motivate you to make the right choices or the correct decisions? Have you ever listened to yourself talk out loud and realize that your words are something less than the truth? I am not accusing anyone of lying. Most people tend to express themselves verbally with half-truths and untruths. It is human nature. We don't want to be judged too harshly by others or be pitied for a physical problem we might have. So what we tend to do is make our situation sound better than it is. Not getting at the heart of the matter causes stress.

Have you noticed that when you journal in the Mind Diet format, your thoughts and words have a simple honesty that allows you to speak the truth? I have no logical explanation for this magical flow, but it happens and it allows your heart and mind to begin to sing. This is a sign that your stress level is decreasing, along with your chances of becoming ill.

Exercise

Here is an exercise I'd like both of you to do before continuing with the book. I want each of you to make a list of the things you've dreamt about that you'd like to accomplish, beginning today. It could be an exotic trip you've wanted to take or an art class or simply painting a room. It is important to list everything you want in your life, just as if cancer had never been a part of it.

1.
2.
3.
4.
5.
6.
7.
8.
9.
10.

I hope this chapter will show you how to let your heart and mind sing about your fears, anxieties, tensions, depressions, and most of all, the cancer; thereby allowing you to once again dream so hope can fill your heart. Read the poems and stir up some positive emotions.

Have Another Day

You owe it to yourself
to get up and start your day;
it's never really that awfully bad.

If you blink or inhale
or just look around, your day
has begun something that's new.
So make an effort to have another day
it's the best that you can do.

Go feel your pain, express your sorrow
and shout a nasty curse,
but don't give up this day you have
that's a decision that will really hurt.

Make a plan to say kind words
to all who are in your life
and make yourself look oh so pretty
to show that you're going to fight.

So have another day again
and plan it very well
and watch the days turn into years
as your attitude moves out of your living hell.

Personal Feelings

Seeing Things From New Eyes

My ghosts swim within my head,
they keep me in a funk,
they scare me throughout my day,
making me act in a dizzy drunk.

I have a past that deals with a future
that is still unknown to me.
I make decisions that just don't seem to work
and it drains the hell out of me.

I am afraid to change and learn,
the fear twists out of control inside my head,
and I wish I had the strength to see
a new way to get out of bed.

I know that I will have to rethink
of how my eyes should see
and try to change the past of how
I thought my life should be.

With eyes opened wide
and thoughts loosened up
I'll begin to see things clear
and use new eyes to process my pain
with a happy song that I can hear.

I want my friends, my lover too,
to join in and walk by my side
and see my world through my new eyes
and show me all their pride.

Personal Feelings

A New Me

I have cancer. I am a survivor.
I fight each day to stay alive.
It is the life that's been made for me
to cherish while it's by my side.

I call myself "The New Me"
it's the old one with reality well in check
and move each day doing things I like to play
with the goal of having no regrets.

A new me does not mean it will exclude
the people that I love.
It just means that I want to share
the vision of survival
that fits me like a glove.

So put on your running shoes
and stretch you heart to go
a new and wonderful ride will follow
toward the only goal I have to survive.

I like the new me, it suits me right,
it feeds and nourishes my soul,
so please decide to take this ride
and watch my new life unfold.

Personal Feelings

Which Life Shall I Choose?

I've been given a new beginning,
in a world that once held me,
and have so many choices to make,
it is so hard for me to believe.

Yesterday I thought of death,
I thought of no future for me,
but now I have a new chance to make
a new life that's right for you to see.

Which life shall I choose?
The answer is easy to make.
I will choose the life that lets me move forward,
and show the world I am a survivor
that has goals she's shooting for.

My wake-up call came way too soon,
it forced me to think real hard
and gave me the choice to look death in the eye
teaching me how I had to survive.

I don't know exactly what life I'll choose,
but believe me I'll try a lot of things
and enjoy the time I have in my life
experimenting as my heart begins to sing.

But understand the real life I want
is to be a survivor that lives many years
and to share each day with the people I love
shedding all my joyful tears.

Personal Feelings

Please Be There For Me

Our lives have changed in many ways
since cancer knocked at our door.
We're not the same two people that dreamed
of a future that we'd adore.

I have no control of the emotions that brew
each day that I work to survive,
but please be there for me with all your heart
as I struggle and fight to stay alive.

I can do this alone, I have the strength
and can beat this poison I have,
but I'd do it better knowing you're by my side
helping to not be so very sad.

I want you there to hold me tight,
to caress away my fears
and I'll take in your loving efforts
as they mix with my fearless tears.

Please be there for me and see me true
and remember our wonderful years
and share with me your thoughts and fears
and even your hidden tears.

Personal Feelings

I Am Normal As Normal Can Be

What you see is what you get,
it's me with a distorted shell.
Some parts are gone or have been removed
that put me in this living hell.

But understand my brain's intact,
it's a little bit out of sorts,
but I am still the woman you know
no matter how much we both hurt.

I am normal as normal can be
under the circumstances I face each day
so don't give up on what we have,
we just have to learn new games to play.

Please hold me tight and compare what you feel
with what was in our past,
and look me in the eyes real deep
to see the woman that's here to last.

I treasure my life the way it is today
and will love you more as my time moves on
and I will try to be as normal as I can
while I sing many different songs.

I need you more than ever before
to keep loving me with all your heart.
So don't let my cancer defeat our relationship.
It is not worth us breaking apart.

Personal Feelings

Each Day Matters

I think in minutes since I've been struck
with the cancer that entered me one day.
I finally understand my time
is too precious to throw away.

Each day does matter, they mean so much,
when death comes knocking at your door
and understand I need each day
to have tomorrows that will help me soar.

I have no number or crystal ball
to know when my candle will go out
and that is why I'm living each day,
enjoying what my life is all about.

So I will make each day matter,
so I can be here for awhile
and hope you'll share my joy for life
and show me your beautiful smile.

Personal Feelings

I Wouldn't Have Missed This For The World

I see my life with wondrous eyes,
with hope for a future for me,
and will appreciate all that I've had
if this cancer finally wins and takes over me.

I wouldn't have missed it for the world
to have the life I've been dealt
and will show no regrets for me
and realize my time's been well spent.

I treasure each day that I've had so far
and will love the ones I have left,
but don't you ever think I'll be angry
if tomorrow my days are spent.

I really mean it when I say,
I've loved each day I've been alive,
and hope you'll remember the good times we had
when I'm no longer alive.

So while I'm here, please go along
with what I want to do
and let's get very playful with our lives
it's the best thing that we can do.

Personal Feelings

My Life is a Rainbow

I wake each day,
my colors have been made anew,
I appreciate the air I breathe.
My life is painted like a rainbow
that shows my new attitude.

I will admit some days are blue
or maybe black as black can be,
but I keep struggling to find the colors
that will be right each day for me.

Those are the days that I can feel my strength,
the power that moves me on
and I keep painting pastel colors
that say I'm getting along.

I see my life as a rainbow,
with hope and faith so bright
and carry with me my special brush
to make each day come out all right.

Personal Feelings

Living All My Dreams in This Life

I can remember my youthful dreams
that gave me hope and strength
and I never questioned that in my life
they would ever get rearranged.

My cancer came like a swirling wind
and twisted me all about
and tried to take my dreams away
by trying to toss them all out.

I am not who I once had been
or whom I thought I'd be,
but I will keep on having dreams
that's how it has to be.

I promise that no matter what
my life will be each day
that I will live my dreams with hope
that I will always get to play.

I want to share my dreams with you
and hear the dreams you have
and try to make one dream for us
that keeps us from being sad.

Personal Feelings

Personal Feelings

Section 7

THE SURVIVOR AND THE SPOUSE

I hope by now that a lot of tears have been shed between the two of you. (I cried as I wrote these poems.) As the spouse of a survivor, it is of utmost importance that you peel back the layer of skin that prevents you from expressing the very emotions that the survivor feels every moment of her day.

Compassion and empathy is only one combination that you need to express daily in order to be of assistance. Patience and time will be asked of you as long as you care to support the cancer survivor in your life.

A lot of demands and work will be required of you if you are going to be the unbending tree that will need to remain strong during the tornado of emotions that will come your way.

My thoughts for the survivor are numerous. It has been said that you can get more from people with a little sweetness. However, bitterness probably consumes your thoughts almost every day. In fact, you might not even know what your true feelings are during your recovery period.

One thing for sure is that you have someone who is willing to learn what is needed to help you through this most horrifying time. Don't expect your spouse to read your mind. Speak to him using the exact words you want him to hear.

What I ask is not without compassion and understanding for what you are going through. I experienced it with my wife, Nancy. However, I was lucky. I didn't wait for her to communicate her fears to me; I came to her first with my poems. I watched her cry deep sobs as uncontrollable, irrational emotions consumed her as she read each of the poems that are in Book One of this series.

I wanted to help Nancy, but had never experienced anyone close to me being ill, especially with a disease that is known to kill. I am not unusual or gifted with wisdom, but rather I have a different way of looking at the life I've been dealt. I always want to be able to celebrate the things around me and to see my world from happy eyes. I love my wife and would do anything in my power to be there for her.

I ask both of you to see your life today and try to find some celebration in what you've been dealt. If you were not communicative before cancer knocked on your door, try to find a way to open up and let your feelings flow into each other's hearts. Seek professional help if needed.

Only two things can happen while you both go through recovery. You'll either go into remission or you will continue to struggle to survive with some very harsh treatments. Either way you need to rewrite your marriage script and become each other's best friends.

Make each day count. Don't miss any opportunity to say, "I love you." Show your love in the form of a rhythm poem.

The following poems are based on interviews I had with female cancer survivors who were not well supported by their spouses. Some of the poems are from the spouse's point of view and others from the survivor's. Finish this last chapter of journaling by reaching the deepest and darkest depths of your emotional soul. Don't hold anything back.

When both of you can accomplish the open and honest communication that is the goal of the Mind Diet journaling program, then the truest Mind Diet will bless both of you and your life together.

Exercise

Make a list of all the things you love about your partner since reaching this point in the book. Be specific and honest.

1.
2.
3.
4.
5.
6.
7.
8.
9.
10.

I'm Afraid to Understand

How can I feel when I don't see my future,
when my mind spins out of control?
I try to appear strong when the pain cuts through me,
but my tears come like a waterfall.

I can't get the fear to escape me right now,
it torments and tears me apart.
I want to be strong and free from my feelings,
but I'm afraid I'll fall apart.

It is not just this cancer
that consumes my thoughts
or the possibility that death is nearby
or that my life is lost.

It is the fear of loneliness each day
as I struggle alone to be alive.
I'm afraid to understand what's happened
as I pray to stay alive.

I can't ask or force you to be a rock,
when your life is falling apart.
I just want us to be able to speak
and not keep our emotions apart.

Let's cuddle right now
and touch and caress
and remember the love that we have
and begin to talk about the feeling we have
that is making us feel oh, so bad.

Personal Feelings

How am I Supposed to Love You?

I see the fear in your eyes,
I sense your terror flow,
I want to hold you very tight
and never let you go.

I just don't know how to help
or how to be there for you.
I just want some objective answers,
to know just what to do.

You were the nurturer of our life,
the caregiver that comforted me,
but now I must give back to you
a part that I am unable to see.

How am I supposed to love you?
I'm confused as I watch you change.
I want the woman that I once had
and for everything to be the same.

Please guide me and have patience
as I try to become real strong
and know that I will do my best
as we struggle to move on.

I am not sure how to love you now
or how to care for you,
or how to be the husband that is strong
and will always follow through.

I'll promise to let you lean on me
and let you cry out loud
and I won't walk away from you
to hide amongst the crowd.

I might not know how to love you now,
but I will begin to understand
and wait to hear your loving words
that will let me be your man.

Personal Feelings

Personal Feelings

I'm Afraid of Losing You

I see your looks, your quietness,
and your back when I'm in my pain.
I hurt inside, not from my recovery,
but your attitude that shows your shame.

I'm sorry I'm not healthy
like I once had been with you,
but I can't change what's happened to me,
so tell me, what you'd like me to do.

I feel so bad that my body and looks
have dwindled from what you bargained for,
but my heart is still the same it was
before the cancer knocked at our door.

I'm afraid of losing you and seeing our life,
evaporate and melt away.
I am not begging you to stick around
or wanting you if you can't play.

I've found a strength that builds in me
each day I am alive
and hope that you'll be there with me
to watch me grow and survive.

I will admit our marriage has changed
and grown away from what it was,
but I believe it is a better one
if you care to get on board.

I am so afraid of losing you,
the love that we once had
and want to show you a new me
so you won't have to remain so sad.

Personal Feelings

I Want It Fixed

The doctors have given you a clean bill of health,
you seem so normal to me,
but I can tell you're way too different
from the woman I used to see.

I want it fixed, for it all to be the same,
as it was before your disease,
and go back to how our love had been
so I can once again believe.

I see your smiles, your energy,
the glow inside your eyes,
but I can see that it's not meant for me
as you struggle to survive.

I want it fixed. I don't know what to do.
I'm confused each day I'm with you
and want the life I had before,
before I became so blue.

I feel we've drifted so far apart,
that a bridge has tumbled down
and that our marriage won't ever be the same
or if I'll ever belong.

Please tell how to get it back.
I miss the times we've had.
I want to try to be there for you
and not feel very sad.

Please hold me close and whisper in my ear
that our life will improve real soon.
I need that reassurance from you
to see my life once again start to bloom.

Personal Feelings

I'm Not Sure I Can Help You

I feel inadequate, helpless, and confused,
trapped knowing I have to perform.
I am not sure I can help you now
or how I need to belong.

I don't know how to be your caregiver
or how to nurture your soul
or how to juggle the life I see each day
that makes me feel alone.

I am not ready to give up on us.
I hope this is a start for me.
Please show me patience for a while
that's just how it has to be.

I'm torn between what I had dreamed
would be a life without sorrow or pain
and now that it has entered my heart
I'm not sure I can start over again.

I hate that cancer has entered our lives
and I hate that it's hurt you so.
I just don't know how to help you now
this torment is hard to let go.

I need some guidance, some answers now
to allow me to change like you
and then I think I'll be able to become
the one who can take care of you.

Personal Feelings

Where Do I Fit In?

I see you struggle with your fight,
with death that is on your mind.
But how can I be there for you?
I feel there's not enough time.

You seek a kinship from other survivors,
from strangers that share with you.
But how can I compete for your attention?
It seems so hard to do.

Where do I fit in?
It is a question
I ask myself each day
and struggle with my mixed-up emotions
while you seem to drift away.

I want to get inside your thoughts,
get deep within your soul
and feel the pain that consumes you so,
so I can truly know.

I want to fit in and understand
what this cancer has done to you,
and hold you close to my aching heart
to help us muddle through.

Please make some room within your heart,
I want to climb inside
and go around with you each day,
no matter where you try to hide.

Personal Feelings

Will Our Lives Ever be the Same?

Since our lives were struck with cancer
nothing has been the same.
We both seem silent and confused
as we search to find something to blame.

Our eyes retain a sadness
that we both had never seen,
while we wait each day for the magic
that once we had always seen.

Our lives don't seem the same
as the dark clouds hover above
and our minds seem to drift toward death
as we remain silent, afraid to move on.

Do we want our lives to be the same
as it was before cancer entered our minds
or do we want to find the way
to change and understand?

Our lives have forever changed,
cancer will never be gone from us.
And we just have to find a new and happy way
to love and gently touch.

Personal Feelings

I Feel Helpless

I don't what to do or say
I feel helpless when I first awake.
I want to hold you close to me,
but my aching heart gets in the way.

I once felt strong in a world
that treated me as a friend,
but now I don't know what to do
or how to try to pretend.

I feel helpless and confused,
my life is out of sorts
and I just want my fear to end
and never come here any more.

Please work with me and guide me toward
a strength that I can't see
and hold my hand so very tight
that's how I want it to be.

Can we work together
to relieve our fear and sorrows?
And take away what's consuming us
and give us positive tomorrows?

Let's make our helpless thoughts disappear
so we won't seem oh so lost
and work together to try to change
our twisted, horrible thoughts.

Personal Feelings

I Miss the Old You

I remember the day when we first met
and the way we fell in love
and how our dreams melted together
as we became one sacred love.

Our future seemed very bright,
we planned for future years,
but now a poison has entered your body
and brought us both to tears.

I miss the old you,
the happy and positive soul
and how you used to care for me
as we planned on getting old.

What will become of the dreams we had
and the life we planned to have?
And what about the laughter, now
that our life has turned so sad?

I really miss the dreams we had,
the long life that you promised me,
and all the hope our future held
in a marriage that was meant to be.

I need your help to see the future,
so share what's in your head,
to understand how you see your life now
that it's not turned out all so sad.

Please talk to me and let me in
to walk within your shoes,
so I can understand you best,
when you are feeling blue.

Personal Feelings

I Don't Know You Anymore

I see your looks, the pity ones,
the impatience that you have
and wish you'd understand my pain
and not come across so mad.

I thought you loved me no matter what
and would be there during our hard times
and never turn your back on me
when I need some private time.

I don't know you anymore,
you seem so distant and aloof,
you keep your thoughts inside your head
with terrible, bothersome moods.

I need to have a partner
who can be strong when I am weak
and hold me in his arms real tight
when the mood says not to speak.

Don't drift away because I'm ill
or because I cry a lot.
I'm telling you I need your strength
and don't want us to give up.

Please show me that you care for me
and reveal the love I used to know,
so I can see the man I knew
with feelings that want to show.

Personal Feelings

I Like What I See

At first I saw death blanket you
and then it consumed my heart
and I tried to remain strong,
but instead fell apart.

I watched you struggle through all your pain,
through the changes that needed to come
and saw a woman so strong and powerful
determined to keep moving on.

There were many times I wanted to run,
to be alone within my pain,
but I just sat and watched you fight
to try to remain so sane.

You are an example of how a person
should handle horrible strife,
the pride you've shown to everyone
that you wanted to save your life.

I've been silent about what I've seen
and how you've struggled and fought
and all I can say is that I am proud
that you haven't really lost.

I'm proud of what I see in you,
it's a strength I wish I had,
and I will stay real close to you
to learn how to handle so much bad.

Personal Feelings

Personal Feelings

A New Beginning

From adversity comes a celebration—if you truly believe it can happen. You will again see your marriage with passion, not passivity. It will not be easy to follow the Mind Diet journaling techniques, but nothing worthwhile in life ever comes easily.

Now that you've completed this journaling program you are well on your way toward a new beginning. You should start to see your marriage with new eyes and your partner the way you did when you first fell in love with him/her.

Having a new beginning in life is something to treasure. A lot of people never get second chances or even the opportunity to start a relationship fresh, without any dirty laundry.

Realize that both of you are unlike any other team. You have a special, loving quality that goes deeper than what you had before. You are the "Survivor and the Spouse Team" and will remain so for as long as you both keep the promise you both sign at the end of this book and continue to write your feelings openly and honestly.

Remember, it is the process not the product that the Mind Diet journaling program strives for. That is what you should set as your goal each and every day you are together.

Thank you for sharing my personal thoughts and poems. I hope they trespassed upon your heart, mind, and most of all your spirit, with the openness and love I had intended.

The marriage agreement on the next page is to be written by both of you. I suggest you first create one individually and then show each other what you would like. Then you can, as a team, come up with a workable agreement that is acceptable to both of you.

New Marriage or Relationship Agreement

I agree to the above marriage/relationship commitment.

Survivor

Spouse/Significant Other

Date

Date

Acknowledgments

I want to thank all the cancer survivors who were brave enough to share their sorrows and pains during their recovery from illness. This book would not have been possible without your honesty and candor about how your worlds have changed since cancer entered your lives. For those who have lost their marriages, I am sorry. You have shown me that being a survivor is not just battling an illness. It is also fighting to keep your life on track, regardless of the odds and obstacles are that are placed in your path.

I also want to thank three very special people who brought to my attention the serious problems married women face when they get cancer. First, thank you to Wendi Vierra, PhD, who first brought to my attention the serious struggles married couples face when cancer enters their lives. And thank you to Nancy Raymond, RN, MN, AOCN and Donna Farris, LCSW, the founders of Healing Odyssey, a support group for cancer survivors.

www.ingramcontent.com/pod-product-compliance
Lightning Source LLC
Chambersburg PA
CBHW032054080426
42733CB00006B/263